philanthropy

&

rural america

COUNCIL *on* FOUNDATIONS

Vision

The Council's vision for the field is of

A vibrant, growing, and responsible philanthropic sector that advances the common good.

We see ourselves as part of a broad philanthropic community that will contribute to this vision. We aim to be an important leader in reaching the vision.

Mission

The Council on Foundations provides the opportunity, leadership and tools needed by philanthropic organizations to expand, enhance, and sustain their ability to advance the common good.

To carry out this mission, we will be a membership organization with effective and diverse leadership that helps the field be larger, more effective, more responsible, and more cooperative.

By *common good* we mean the sum total of conditions that enable community members to thrive. These achievements have a shared nature that goes beyond individual benefits.

By *philanthropic organizations* we mean any vehicle that brings people together to enhance the effectiveness, impact and leverage of their philanthropy. This includes private and community foundations, corporate foundations and giving programs, operating foundations, and public foundations, as well as emerging giving and grantmaking mechanisms involving collective participation.

Statement of Inclusiveness

The Council on Foundations was formed to promote responsible and effective philanthropy. The mission requires a commitment to inclusiveness as a fundamental operating principle and calls for an active and ongoing process that affirms human diversity in its many forms, encompassing but not limited to ethnicity, race, gender, sexual orientation, economic circumstance, disability, and philosophy. We seek diversity in order to ensure that a range of perspectives, opinions, and experiences are recognized and acted upon in achieving the Council's mission. The Council also asks members to make a similar commitment to inclusiveness in order to better enhance their abilities to contribute to the common good of our changing society.

Philanthropy & Rural America was edited by Doug Rule.

COUNCIL *on* FOUNDATIONS
2121 Crystal Drive, Suite 700
Arlington, VA 22202
703-879-0600 • Fax 703-879-0800
www.cof.org

Why a Journal on Rural Philanthropy?

Stereotypes and misperceptions muddle our views of rural America. Typically conceived as wide-open spaces and small, close communities, rural America as a region is rarely painted as progressive and forward-thinking. Yet by its very nature, it has been. Rural areas were the first to experience and adapt to the Great Depression, some 10 years before its full impact registered across the nation. More recently, rural America was the first to bear the brunt of globalization, a still-emerging phenomenon in which no one nation—and especially, no one region—can expect to survive and thrive alone; in which no one can expect their traditions to see them through.

In fact, today's rural America, though vastly different from yesterday's, remains every bit as much a bellwether of challenges the rest of America will face tomorrow as it ever was. It stands to reason, then, that rural America can also become an incubator of promising new ideas to help with those challenges. Rural residents are hard at work to help retool and revive their communities altered by population changes, environmental pressures, economic demands, educational needs and more. And philanthropy has a perfect opportunity to help.

This journal, the first in a new series of journals on relevant topics for the field of philanthropy from the Council on Foundations, was designed to capture some of the best ideas from some of the best minds in philanthropy already engaged in helping rural America. Working independently and especially together, foundations everywhere can help to further implement these ideas. In every corner of the country, foundations can, and should, lead the way to a better tomorrow. You will quickly see the diversity of thought—including criticism of philanthropy and the Council. In an era of honest conversations, transparency, and a commitment to philanthropic leadership we welcome these thoughts, even when they make us uncomfortable.

Steve Gunderson

Going Home Again:
A Personal Vision of Rural America in 2015

It was a beautiful Saturday evening in late June. Hundreds of people had filled the main street of my hometown of Osseo, Wisconsin, celebrating the community's 150th anniversary. With the music of a dance band behind us, the conversations were as free-flowing as the beers—a Wisconsin tradition! Soon one of the voices at my table inquired whether I would ever consider moving home.

The question was warm and kind—almost an invitation to find the path from my present work at the Council on Foundations back home to my roots. If the path didn't happen this year, or next, or even in the distant future, it was clear the open invitation would be there whenever my professional life might consider such an offer. One is always welcome back home!

A couple of years ago, a sister and her family made such a decision. Having raised two of their three children in Madison, they decided to come home. Through technology she is able to continue her professional work as the owner of a small business. Her husband's work is global in nature, much of it focused on international trade with China. Airports, telephones and technology define his work—not the size or location of his hometown.

Their move home defines a positive vision for rural America's future. They are able to combine their professions and daily work within the values of small-town life. From the pride of high school sports to the introspection of their church, from service in the volunteer fire department to increased fellowship with extended family, they are constructing a 21st century portrayal of rural American life. Their work is not defined by an eight-to-five presence at the office, but rather upon the utilization of advanced technology and communications. It is their job skills, not the location of their work, that matters. They are self-employed. They work hard, but their hours are flexible. They live in small-town rural America, but they operate on a national—or even global—scale.

Rural America in Transition

For 16 years (1980 to 1996), I had the honor of representing western Wisconsin in the halls of the United States Congress. True to my district's needs I focused my work on agriculture, education and constituent service. In some unique ways, with 16 rural counties and hundreds of local municipalities, I was the de-facto mayor of my congressional district. One of my most important contributions in preparing rural western Wisconsin for the future was my organization of annual economic development conferences around the theme "Western Wisconsin 2000." We recognized the change among us. And we needed to create the vision for our future.

These conferences focused on change. They sought to introduce western Wisconsin to the pace and magnitude of change in the years ahead. We brought in futurists to discuss everything from new production methods in agriculture to the reality of the emerging global economy. And we prefaced almost every aspect of change by advocating for a new public-private partnership. But we never once discussed philanthropy.

Were I to organize such a conference today, it would be called "Western Wisconsin 2020." And philanthropy would be a critical element of the program's focus. I would recognize that family farms are no longer a way of life, but a profession. I'd admit that unskilled rural manufacturing has been exported and replaced by the same high-skill demands of our urban neighbors. We would look for ways to sell the attraction of open space and the benefits of our rural environment. We would talk about technology, distance education and the web as essential components of our infrastructure—not some ideal but expensive option. We would look at integrated health care delivery, and a new focus on healthy lifestyles built on homegrown produce and the consumer's preference for organic products. We'd talk about the merger of our financial institutions and the changing nature of financial capital in rural America. Finally, we'd look at the need for new sources and types of rural equity financing.

But we'd remember the words of Susan Berresford, outgoing President of the Ford Foundation, when she explains, "We invest in rural America because we find that rural America is so innovative in its response to the challenges it faces. We can all learn from them—even in our largest urban areas."

Rural America is not only the home of innovation, it is also a place where leadership is a necessity—not an option. At the Council on Foundation's first-ever conference on rural philanthropy organized last August, Montana Governor Brian Schweitzer said that rural areas are where America has cultivated its leaders for centuries. Referencing his own path to becoming a rising star in his Democratic party, Schweitzer said that philanthropy could work to help nurture "another poor kid from a small town in a rural state who may become the next governor." Without philanthropy's help, though, the same kid might not realize his full leadership potential.

And without philanthropy's help, rural America itself might not realize its full potential—potential for innovative solutions to problems that vex us all. But philanthropy must act now. Rural America, already vastly different than it was just 13 years ago, will be just as different 13 years later. Rural Americans' average income continues to lag behind that of its urban brothers. The days when the sale of one's farm provided Mom and Dad with their retirement security is also gone. The merger of small-town independent banks has eroded the local banker's investment in his neighbor as an entrepreneur.

If I were giving the opening remarks at Western Wisconsin 2020, I would offer the following vision for rural America:

- Immigration and diversity will describe rural America's population just as it now defines our urban centers.

- Technology will define rural America's ability to participate in the global economy.

- Skilled workers will determine which rural communities prosper in a knowledge-based economy. Workforce skills, not work habits, will mark the difference between prosperity and poverty.

- Infrastructure needs will challenge rural America—from transportation to communication. Our ability to connect to the rest of the world will determine our ability to participate in a 24/7 economy.

- An appreciation for the arts, an environmental ethic, and a commitment to community creativity—in every sense of that term—will define our values.

Richard Florida's pioneering work articulates the role of creativity in a community's future. At the Council's 2006 annual conference, Florida, a professor at George Mason University, noted that already one-third of the American workforce makes a living in what he calls the fast-growing creative economy, which includes industries of science and technology, education and entrepreneurship, and arts and culture. "In order to grow, in order to be prosperous, in order to compete, we can only find one asset: the further development of human creative capabilities," Florida said. For any place to successfully stem a brain drain of residents moving for more creative, intellectually stimulating work elsewhere, the key, according to Florida, is to harness creativity by making jobs of all kinds more rewarding; by working to change the economy to bene-fit employees as well as employers. Also essential is to override a community's "squelchers," or people who resist change and see it as a threat, not the promise it should be.

The Potential for Rural Philanthropy

Yet, change—and the management of change towards a positive outcome—requires resources. I suspect the investment in philanthropy today will define our resources for tomorrow.

In 2001, the Nebraska Community Foundation used the Boston College study "Millionaires in the Millennium" to develop the metrics necessary to envision the potential for new philanthropy in its state. The Foundation estimated that by 2050, $94 billion in wealth will be transferred among generations of Nebraskans. The question yet to be answered is how much of this will be directed towards philanthropy providing long-term, on-going sources of support for the common good.

In my home state, the Wisconsin Donors Forum contracted with the Nebraska Community Foundation to use its metrics to predict Wisconsin's transfer of wealth. The conclusion: "Wisconsin will experience an estimated $687 billion in inter-generational transfer" in the next 50 years. Trempealeau County, my home county of 27,000 people, will witness a transfer of wealth in the next 10 years of $320 million—averaging over $42,000 per household. And these numbers are less than 70 percent of the state-wide average because of our distinct rural demographics.

But imagine: If just 5 percent of the $320 million in Trempealeau County's genera-tional transfer of wealth were captured by local community philanthropy, we would create an endowment of $16 million. Using the 5 percent payout of private foundations as our guide, this would provide $800,000 in annual support for local programs serving the common good of our rural county.

Rural America will continue to define charity. Every day and every week, rural residents give in disproportionate ways to support the needs of their neighbors. Rural churches consistently show much higher donations per capita than those in urban areas. Rural nonprofits survive by the constant and innovative support of local residents. Rich and timely, these charitable gifts reflect our giving of the heart and for the moment. We celebrate this value.

But philanthropy is different. Philanthropy is, by definition, a long-term strategic investment of our charitable resources for the public good. It is, or should be, the architect of social change—not just responding to immediate needs and problems but also searching for ways to solve them once and for all. Zoltan Acs, a professor at George Mason University, has written that the distinction between charity and philanthropy is similar to that between small business and entrepreneurship. "Small business is about lifestyle and entrepreneurship is about wealth creation. In the same sense, charity is about redistribution while philanthropy in the American tradition is about investing wealth to create opportunity."

Philanthropy, as a sector, is one growth area in America that will continue to flourish. While the private and public sectors will face new limitations in their ability to contribute to the common good, philanthropy is bound to grow in size and in service. The combination of demographics and resources suggest we might be at the beginning of a new golden age in philanthropic growth.

American business is focused on survival in a global economy. Though corporate social responsibility plays an increasing part in its activities, by necessity it must defer to larger interests than those of one area or even region, especially rural. American government, meanwhile, has largely turned power into paralysis. Though our needs in rural America are arguably greater now than ever, the response from government at all levels is increasingly limited and inept, armed with a one-size-fits-all mentality that is the opposite of what's needed. Philanthropy, on the other hand, is able to work with differences, embrace radical solutions, take risks—even fail—and then try again. Philanthropy is the one sector fully capable of innovating solutions—but it won't happen without a serious commitment to doing so.

While it is the one sector with the greatest potential, philanthropy must work with business and government if it truly hopes to help rural America meet its needs. Cross-sector partnerships are critical. Work to improve the economy, jobs and the workforce, education and the environment are just a few of the many areas in which all sectors have vested interests—and where no sector can hope to achieve real progress alone. Though government has shirked much of its duties over the past few decades, it's important that government officials and policymakers realize that they still bear a burden of responsibility to help, a burden they can't simply transfer to others, including philanthropy.

There are also clear ways government can help philanthropy better serve society. An era of public-philanthropic partnerships is emerging in multiple ways. First, Congress creates the environment in which philanthropy can grow and prosper. Tax laws, tax incentives and IRS regulations will determine whether individuals are willing and able to invest their resources in philanthropy. In defining new parameters for partnership, Congress is looking at ways in which philanthropy and public dollars partner for economic development through the new Farm Bill, and partner in providing new opportunities for post-secondary education through the Higher Education Act. Such partnerships would have not been considered even five years ago. They may represent a new era of cooperation, partnership and investment.

Congress and State Legislatures can also help address the financial capital needs of rural America through the passage of legislation allowing foundations to make program-related grants or loans to "low-profit liability companies," like a community newspaper, and have it count toward the federal requirement that private foundations distribute at least 5 percent of their assets each year. Such a company would function to earn modest profits while conducting business for the public good, with profits returned to the community through additional grants.

Creating the Rural Philanthropic Partnership

We must harness this philanthropic potential in many ways. First, many of our rural citizens have grown up and moved to the city and suburbs where they have successful careers. We need them to bring some of their philanthropic investments back home. Even more important, we must increase awareness among them and among society at large about rural America's needs—about how a little help can go a long way. Foundations need to hear success stories and ways in which rural communities work together and ways in which foundations can make, and are making, a difference.

There is a substantial cultural and geographic disconnect between foundations and rural communities. According to the Center for Rural Strategies, because most foundations are based in urban areas and managed by urban dwellers, "out of sight does mean out of mind." Foundations around the country are leading promising efforts to connect urban donors with rural nonprofits. As you'll read in this journal, Alaska's Rasmuson Foundation invites national funders on an Educational Tour of Alaska for Grantmakers. Eleven years after the first tour, the Foundation's Diane Kaplan says over $50 million has been raised for rural Alaskan nonprofits from these out-of-state funders. The Anschutz Family Foundation in Colorado, meanwhile, has worked to engage more in-state foundation support for rural areas through its Rural Philanthropy Days. Twice a year, various foundation leaders visit the state's rural communities to better understand their issues and challenges. As a result, the Foundation's Jeffrey Pryor says philanthropic support to rural locations in the state has increased over the past decade from totaling just 3 percent to 15 percent. These are remarkable stories, because they point to ways to increase philanthropy through positive, voluntary means.

Second, we must recognize the importance of building a new generation of philanthropic infrastructure in our rural communities. There are many innovative structures being designed to serve this need. We need to embrace and support all of them. Janet Topolsky of the Aspen Institute provides a fine overview of developments in her essay in this journal. Elsewhere, you'll read about efforts, such as the McKnight Foundation's pioneering Minnesota Initiative Foundations, to establish more community foundations serving rural communities. These efforts are so exciting because they are helping rural communities become self-sufficient, in control of their own destinies. Also noteworthy are efforts, such as the Community Foundation of South Wood County in Wisconsin, to engage citizens in building on existing resources to strengthen the local economy, create an entrepreneurial culture and plan for the future.

Third, the value of collaboration among foundations cannot be overstated. Philanthropies of all sizes and stripes should collaborate more, adding their own expertise toward tackling a common interest or problem. Working in partnership with others who bring to bear their own experience in an area is key. It may be a cliché, but it's worth repeating: There is *real* power in partnership. Foundations can work to strengthen intermediaries.

Fourth, we must recognize this window of opportunity is immediate. In the Nebraska Community Foundation's work within their own state, they have determined that no less than 25 percent of their rural counties will experience the intergenerational transfer of wealth within the next six years due to the aging of their population. This is not an opportunity we can put off until tomorrow.

It's why the Council convened its first rural philanthropy conference less than a year into our Rural Philanthropy project. It's why we're issuing this journal, to help keep the ideas alive. It's why we've established an Advisory Committee on Philanthropy and Rural America, and why we'll host a second conference early next year, to check on our progress toward increasing philanthropy's help for rural America. We realize there is urgency in the matter—that rural America can't wait until we're ready.

In fact, Karl Stauber, formerly of the Northwest Area Foundation, has written that the next few years are critical. In a 2004 paper for federal policymakers, Stauber notes that some rural areas have lost so much population—especially people in their "maximum earnings" years, ages 19 to 64—and so much economic activity that further decline puts their very survival at significant risk. "Population loss, economic decline and increasing poverty emphasize the need to move swiftly in developing new policies for rural America," he writes. Time is of the essence.

Going Home, Again

When Richard Florida spoke to the Council's Annual Conference in Pittsburgh, the theme of the annual gathering was "Investing in the Vision of Progress: Insight, Inspiration, Innovation, and Impact." This same theme continues to serve as our guide for the potential of philanthropy in building rural America's future. We must have the insight to understand the challenges facing rural America's quest towards an enhanced quality of life—and opportunity—for all its citizens. In many ways the barriers to progress are greater than those of our urban colleagues, yet the resources are less. We must also find the inspiration for a vision of what rural America can be. Building upon realistic insight of where we are and idealistic visions of inspiration, we will engage the rural values of inspiration to create new partnerships, new investments, new strategies and real impact.

When I go home, I want to see a $16 million community foundation endowment, providing no less than $800,000 in annual investments, building a new future and enhancing the common good. I want to see my neighbors engaging their skills, their technology and their entrepreneurship in ways that provide incomes comparable to their urban competitors. I want to see a western Wisconsin built on diversity in population and in the economy. I want to see their products—from agriculture to art—as part of the market shelves across the nation, and perhaps the globe. I want to look back, knowing that my personal role in the growth of philanthropy and our common vision for the role of philanthropy made a difference.

J. Irwin Miller is an industrialist in Indiana who created the Cummings diesel engines. In creating his own foundation, he shared a guiding principle with his staff when he said, "Ten years from now, what will you wish you had done today?" This is the challenge—and the opportunity—for rural America. It is also my vision for philanthropy and rural America's future.

Steve Gunderson is President and CEO of the Council on Foundations.

rural america today—
the need for philanthropy

philanthropy

&

rural america

section I

If the celebrated dog Lassie still lives in rural America, he may not be faring so well. There is great diversity, in every sense of the word, in the region today, including even how one defines the term 'rural.' But considered as a whole, rural areas come up more than just short in population relative to urban and suburban regions. Rural areas are also short in philanthropy.

The authors of essays in the first two chapters of this journal include a prominent U.S. Senator, two noted critics of foundation giving, especially for community needs, and several leading practitioners of rural philanthropy—or at least, philanthropy primarily directed toward rural areas. What these authors stress is the need for more such philanthropy. As they report, there's a need to overcome distorting perceptions of rural life, there's a need to help rural communities boost their own philanthropic capacity and strengthen their own philanthropic infrastructure, and there's a need for more communication and collaboration between urban and rural funders.

Philanthropy can help rural areas successfully transform their economies and their cultures as demanded by an increasingly connected world—we're all in it together. If Lassie isn't thriving in his own natural habitat, what hope have we?

CHAPTER 1 |

Why Rural Matters

Bridging the Philanthropic Divide: Building Cooperation, Community and Capacity with Rural America

I learned recently of the story of B. John Barry, a man born and raised in rural North Dakota. Like many Americans from rural areas, he left home in his youth to pursue a big-city career. Over the years, success blessed Mr. Barry. A commitment to sharing his own good fortune led him to found The Barry Foundation in Minneapolis-Saint Paul, Minnesota.

A while after forming that foundation in the Twin Cities, Mr. Barry decided to do something unusual. Having researched and studied philanthropy for many years, Mr. Barry was attuned to the lack of charitable foundation assets in his home state: North Dakota ranks 51st among the 50 states and the District of Columbia for in-state foundation assets. Mr. Barry still felt a strong connection to the rural community where he got his start. For that reason, he and his family committed to giving half the foundation's grants each year to the community of Fargo and to the surrounding region. And in 2006, Mr. Barry and his family decided to move The Barry Foundation's headquarters to Fargo. The family hopes that their example will inspire other foundations to make similar commitments to rural areas.

America's long tradition of philanthropy has been a foundation for our nation's greatness. Advances in health care, help for those in need, and explosions in the creative arts have been sparked by generous giving. But sadly, rural America has missed much of the promise of philanthropy. There is a shortage of assets within rural states, and a scarcity of giving to rural areas. Some call this inequity the "Philanthropic Divide."

In my home state of Montana and in other rural states, foundations frequently have fewer resources. Their endowments are smaller than those of their urban counterparts. According to data released in 2006, Montana's foundation assets totaled $404 million, ranking the state 48th nationally in terms of in-state foundation assets. In that same year, Montana placed 46th nationally for grantmaking by in-state foundations.

Organizations in rural areas also receive less funding from national foundations than projects in urban places. The Big Sky Institute for the Advancement of Nonprofits reports that funding from national foundations to rural states actually declined between 2000 and 2004, from $104 million in 2000 to $96 million in 2004. In 2005, grants nationwide averaged $51.98 for each American. They were $116.35 per capita in New York, and just $33.86 per capita in Montana.

This serious inequity demands a response from all of us. Rural America has contributed richly to the nation's economy and to philanthropy itself, but rural America has never received comparable philanthropic return.

Because foundations benefit from a tax-exempt status, it is incumbent on them to act with fairness and equity. The charitable tax-exemption was intended for the benefit of our entire country, and the philanthropic community should fairly and equitably distribute charitable giving nationwide. And more importantly, philanthropic equality will better reflect the American value of the worth of every citizen.

Eighty-eight percent of persistently poor counties are rural counties. Families headed by hard-working single mothers in rural America are some of the poorest families in our country. Forty-three percent of female-led rural families are poor, compared with 35 percent of their urban counterparts. Rural schools, clinics and food banks need attention. The philanthropic community can address these basic issues in many ways, and can do even more to help rural areas.

In May of 2006, I called on the philanthropic community to double grants to rural states over the next five years. I have continued to encourage foundations to make giving in rural places a priority. Philanthropists from all over the country have voiced their support and commitment for this idea. But as foundations move to invest more of their charitable dollars in rural places, they should do so with four specific goals in mind.

Philanthropic organizations must encourage the development of more rural community foundations, invest in organizations that help rural nonprofits build capacity to help more people, confront the challenges that keep them from making grants to rural organizations in the first place, and partner with everyone from Congress to local organizations to bridge the rural philanthropic divide.

Developing Rural Community Foundations

Community foundations are important because they are operated by decision-makers familiar with local needs, local conditions and local resources. National foundations can help rural community foundations develop by providing grants to help build staffs, grow the organizations and help them become sustainable for generations to come. Investing in the development of local community foundations turns an initial grant into a long-term asset within a community. And it addresses one of the most significant problems in rural philanthropy: the shortage of philanthropic assets in rural states. A powerful infusion of philanthropic support to help start local community foundations in rural regions, and to build up existing ones, can move mountains in rural states.

The Nebraska Community Foundation is helping Nebraskans leave philanthropic legacies through an innovative model that could be replicated in rural areas across the country. Leaders have pioneered a model to harness the power of local community philanthropy in land-rich rural places that generally do not have high per-capita incomes. They are convincing their neighbors to leave just 5 percent of their estates —made up primarily of land—to local community foundations. This will bring in millions of dollars in local community endowments through the transfer of wealth from this generation to the next.

Helping Rural Nonprofits Grow

Organizations that support nonprofits help folks in the charitable community. Large foundations can significantly affect the rural philanthropic divide by investing in groups that provide specialized support for rural nonprofits. National foundations may fund rural state nonprofit associations, give grants for rural technological support services, offer scholarships to degree programs in nonprofit management for rural students, or help rural nonprofits design internship opportunities that attract top-notch students.

The Montana Nonprofit Association has successfully applied these strategies to the benefit of its current membership of 450 nonprofit organizations. For example, the MNA offers far more affordable health insurance coverage for nonprofits' employees than a single nonprofit could purchase for its workers. The MNA has benefited from out-of-state grant support from such foundations as the Otto Bremer Foundation, the Kelley Family Foundation, the Northwest Area Foundation, the Arthur M. Blank Foundation, the M.J. Murdock Charitable Trust and the Steele-Reese Foundation. I applaud these organizations for their support, and encourage more large foundations to assist with similar organizations and programs in rural states.

Facilitating Giving to Rural Communities

A number of challenges constrain national foundations from making grants to rural nonprofit organizations. But foundations must meet those challenges head on—even if they need to revise their funding guidelines to do so. Foundations with guidelines that are in line with the needs of rural organizations can help to build directly the capacities of high-caliber nonprofits, or can provide seed funding and challenge grants to navigate crucial developmental stages.

A better understanding of the realities of rural philanthropy can also lead to more giving. Often, an effective organization in Montana will affect a five- or six-county region with a smaller population than what would be found in an urban center. The larger distance spanned with a smaller population affected may look inefficient by comparison to big-city philanthropy—but it may represent great success in a rural area. This success should be rewarded and built upon. I urge foundations to continue to learn and to develop strategies that will connect rural areas and national funders, and to revise their funding guidelines accordingly.

Building Better Partnerships for Rural Philanthropy

National foundations' greatest effect on rural areas could come through partnering for the good of these regions.

National foundations can work together with Congress on policies that help people in rural areas. For example, I worked hard to improve the Earned Income Tax Credit, which returns hard-earned tax dollars to low-income working families. In turn, nonprofit organizations in Montana have helped more working families utilize the EITC. The Kellogg Foundation partnered with these organizations to help low-income Montanans, many of them living in rural communities, to receive more than a million dollars in tax refunds.

National foundations can also partner directly with local communities. I have worked hard to facilitate cooperation between national foundations and local individuals and organizations in my home state. I have hosted two Faith Community Impact Summits in Montana. The Summit brings faith leaders, nonprofits and community groups together with charitable foundations to work together on pressing community problems. This year's Summit in Kalispell addressed issues like methamphetamine abuse, hunger, housing and environmental stewardship. It was an opportunity for innovative local groups to build relationships with large foundations, so they can work together in the future.

When considering the need for more rural philanthropy, I think about how rural America has always been, and remains, instrumental to the American economy. Whether through timber, mining, oil or steel, or through the railroads that first connected the nation, rural America has been vital to the creation of immense wealth and in turn, great philanthropy.

But it is also true that rural regions have not received a philanthropic investment reflective of their economic contributions. William A. Clark, one of the three "Copper Kings" of Butte, Montana, died in 1925 in his Fifth Avenue mansion in New York City as one of the 50 wealthiest people in American history. His major philanthropic contribution was to the Corcoran Gallery in Washington, D.C., in the form of an art collection so large that the museum constructed an entirely new wing to house it. Similarly, John Jacob Astor made a significant portion of his fortune in the fur-trading industry in the Great Lakes Region and the Pacific Northwest. He invested his fortune in New York real estate and built the Astor Library in that city.

These philanthropists' great gifts of art, culture and libraries in Washington, D.C., and New York City are vital assets in these urban centers and to the entire nation. But their gifts seldom touch the rural areas that provided much of the philanthropic bounty in the first place. So I am glad for a new awareness in the philanthropic community, where leading foundations are remembering their roots.

Michael Benedum, benefactor of the Claude W. Benedum Foundation, was a successful oil and gas entrepreneur from West Virginia who eventually settled in Pittsburgh. In his will, he eloquently noted that Pittsburgh was better off than the rural regions of West Virginia. He devoted his charitable endowment to the people and organizations of rural West Virginia and of southwestern Pennsylvania out of what he called "a sense of equity." The Benedum Foundation has been instrumental in the establishment and growth of numerous community foundations in those regions. And of course, the Barry Foundation's long-term commitment to the state of North Dakota and to the Red River Valley has been an innovative, insightful effort to address rural needs.

Every American philanthropic foundation can learn a lesson from these examples. Rural America has always been willing to contribute to this nation's success. It is time this nation contributed more to the success of rural communities.

Senator Max Baucus has dedicated his life to serving the people of Montana. After serving in the Montana State Legislature, Baucus was elected to the U.S. House of Representatives in 1974. He served there until elected to the U.S. Senate in 1978 and has served there ever since.

L i n d a   R e e d

Debunking the Myths About Rural America:
One Size Does Not Fit All

To people living in urban America, images of rural America range from romantic to depressing. At the romantic end of the spectrum, we conjure up images of open space, beautiful landscapes, an abundant source of food, a strong work ethic and close-knit communities. We are all those things and more.

At the other end, we are viewed as backward, uneducated, poor and underprivileged. How do we survive, after all, without Whole Foods or Urban Outfitters within an hour's drive?

The myths abound, but the reality is that there is no monolithic, one-size-fits-all definition of rural America. When you have seen one rural community, you have seen one rural community. The same undoubtedly applies to urban communities. And in fact, many present-day concerns in rural communities in America are not so different from those facing communities in urban America. These include poverty, poorly funded schools, lack of affordable housing, drug addiction, international competition for jobs, immigration and discrimination, and collapsing public infrastructure.

Rural areas do share some special challenges though. More important, they also offer special opportunities for foundations. By all means, foundations should view rural America as an incubator. Working in true partnership with local nonprofits and foundations, regional and national funders could have serious impact on a small scale in a short span of time, and then take the ideas and lessons learned and import them to other rural areas. Even urban and suburban areas could benefit from the work already being done in rural areas to solve some entrenched social problems affecting us all.

> By all means, foundations should view rural America as an incubator. Working in true partnership with local nonprofits and foundations, regional and national funders could have serious impact on a small scale in a short span of time, and then take the ideas and lessons learned and import them to other rural areas.

Great Diversity in Rural America Demands Better, More Diverse Policy

What is needed among both grantmakers and policymakers is recognition of the great diversity that exists in rural America. Grantmaking initiatives and federal policies will not solve our problems of economic vitality, access to health care, transportation and infrastructure costs, balanced growth and rural poverty if they are implemented in a one-size-fits-all fashion. We can't possibly expect solutions that will work as well in Montana as they do in Arkansas.

In terms of federal policy, going back as far as the Homestead Act of 1862, there have been few initiatives that have helped Montana in the long term. While 160 acres in Kansas or Nebraska may be enough to sustain a family, it is just enough for slow starvation in the arid western states of Montana, Wyoming and Nevada. And the Conservation Reserve Program has saved many acres of sensitive wildlife habitat and actually slowed rural sprawl, but it has been the death knell for many of our small rural communities. Our aging farmers are no longer farming; instead, they are taking their CRP payments and retiring. When farmers are paid not to cultivate their land, less labor is needed for farming, fewer crops are stored in local granaries and fewer implements are replaced or maintained. It's a domino effect: when small businesses directly supported by agriculture fail, other Main Street businesses aren't far behind. The next to go are the schools.

And what about No Child Left Behind? How does that work in a state that has 44 school *districts* each with fewer than 10 students, and 101 *districts* each with fewer than 50? It took Montana school officials three years just to negotiate a workable definition of a "highly qualified teacher" under the federal policy. And where does that leave the one-room schools that still exist in so many rural states? What teacher can be certified in all subjects? And what rural school district could afford that teacher?

Meanwhile, I know there were abuses that needed to be addressed in HR4, the Pension Protection Act of 2006. But the regulations stemming from this legislation have only made our work harder, not better. The average scholarship granted through donor-advised funds at the Montana Community Foundation is $1,200. The administrative overhead now required to grant that scholarship is so burdensome, it barely leaves any funds for distribution. We may have to stop accepting scholarship endowments altogether. In the meantime, we are searching for ways to make our process and oversight more efficient because our students need those scholarships.

In August of 2007, Montana hosted the first-ever Conference on Rural Philanthropy.

Organized by the Council on Foundations, the conference brought nearly 200 philanthropic leaders and grantmakers from throughout the country to address federal policies and philanthropic practices as they relate to rural America. The goal was to create sustained resources for future investment in building community and to build partnerships among the public, private and philanthropic sectors to help meet that goal. It was a thrilling event for us because we were able to showcase the good work going on in Montana by several nonprofit organizations that are addressing some very specific needs. Several task forces were formed during the conference to address specific issues, one of them focused on federal policy. Several ideas came out of that task force that merit closer examination by policymakers, as well as by foundations working to improve federal policy.

One was to support passage of legislation creating a new organizational designation, the L3C, or Limited Liability Low Profit Corporation. This could encourage philanthropic investments in economic development activities in economically depressed areas. Another was to ask Congress to redefine "rural." The term is defined differently in so many federal programs that the programs often cannot serve the constituencies they were designed to help. The most obvious examples are the small rural communities that are located in counties with a metropolitan area large enough to disqualify smaller, outlying communities from receiving federal grants under some program guidelines.

A third policy idea to emerge from the conference in August was the universal deployment of broadband. In Montana, we know how powerful that is because we are fortunate to live in a state that is generally "wired." But it is not a panacea for maintaining rural vitality. I learned from a colleague in North Carolina that broadband was actually closing medical clinics and doctors' offices in rural communities because distances are shorter in North Carolina than they are out West. In the eastern states, you don't have to drive very far to reach an urban center with medical services. As rural clinics use broadband services to access technical expertise, it only encourages patients to develop relationships with physicians in urban areas. That doesn't happen in Montana, where the drive from a rural community to an urban hospital is often more than 100 miles. The disparity between eastern rural and western rural is yet another reminder that when you have seen one rural community, you have seen one rural community.

Philanthropy and the Need for Sustainable Sources of Funding

But what about the role of regional and national philanthropic organizations in meeting the needs of rural America? Again, we must consider the potential with eyes wide open. We cannot trust distant foundations to know what's best for us. Just the opposite is true. Philanthropic decision makers need to trust us to know what's best for our own communities, be they in Montana or Arkansas. As we demonstrated at our August conference, we are on the ground, doing good work that fits the very specific needs of our rural communities. All we lack is a sustainable source of funding.

As demonstrated in the essays included in this journal, foundations with experience helping rural America have learned the importance of adapting their efforts to meet local community needs, based on extensive engagements with local leaders. Time and time again, the take-home message for foundations is the need for local access, even control, of funding. This means helping plan for increased funding in the future, such as the Nebraska Community Foundation's efforts profiled in this journal. It also means helping establish endowed funds for the present and the future, such as the work of the McKnight Foundation and many others. Establishing more local community foundations and donor-advised funds in rural areas is critical to helping these areas thrive.

Statewide community foundations like the Montana Community Foundation are not the norm. We exist as an umbrella foundation for the entire state precisely because our population is so small. With just over 900,000 residents, Montana compares with a mid-size American city, most of which have their own community foundations. We are doing on a smaller scale just what we are asking larger regional and national foundations to consider when it comes to addressing rural needs: Offering incentives to local communities to create their own endowments for future grantmaking in their own communities. Currently, there are 45 local community foundations affiliated with us. In terms of fundraising, building endowment and grantmaking, the most active and effective are the ones in some of Montana's smallest communities. As granters and community conveners, these local foundations are doing remarkable work—building community centers, parks and playgrounds, adding books to library shelves and storage capacity to food banks. It's the kind of work that likely wouldn't have been funded otherwise, since these are needs that outside foundations working alone might not have considered important. But even local foundations can only do so much with limited resources. Clearly, more and greater support is needed.

So we are asking regional and national foundations to trust us to make the right decisions. Trust us to know the greatest needs in each of our very distinct rural communities. We may be poor and underprivileged from an urban perspective, but we have more paved streets than you think, and we have the street smarts to prove it.

Linda Reed is president and CEO of the Montana Community Foundation, a statewide philanthropic organization that works with donors, charitable organizations, cities and towns to promote community vitality and the expansion of endowed philanthropy. The Foundation manages total assets of more than $60 million in permanent endowment funds and distributes more than $2 million a year in grants to charitable organizations and educational scholarships.

CHAPTER 2 |

Rural America—
The Road Not Taken

A a r o n   D o r f m a n

The Power of Persuasion:
Getting More Foundations to Fund Rural

When the Council on Foundations convened a summit on rural philanthropy in Montana in August 2007, about 170 foundation leaders from across the country attended. For an organization whose annual conference draws upwards of 2,000 attendees, the turnout was disappointingly low. The conference's potential value to draw new funders into the fold was lost—the event largely catered to current rural grantmakers.

From what I can tell, the lack of attendance from funders who aren't already committed to funding in rural areas wasn't an accident. The Council knows how to get a good turnout when it wants to, and it could have found a way to interest more than the usual suspects if the goal of the conference was to increase funding for nonprofits providing assistance to rural areas. So what happened? Essentially, it boils down to this: There is an aversion at the Council on Foundations, and throughout the sector, to any serious debate about what causes are worthy of funding and where foundations' priorities should lie. It's as if there is some unwritten rule that says you can't suggest to another foundation what they should do with their money, let alone make a compelling case for a shift in the focus of their grant-making. As a trade association, the Council is especially reluctant to tell its members what to do. Discussion of a redistribution of current dollars has been off the table even as the Council tackles the issue of how to grow new philanthropic resources for rural America.

If we're serious about philanthropy being relevant to the most pressing issues facing our nation, it's time to abandon that unwritten rule and engage in some serious discussions about where philanthropic dollars can do the most good. We won't see a sizable increase in philanthropy for rural areas without putting redistribution of current dollars on the table. The same holds true about the lack of funding for other marginalized groups. Creating African-American giving circles, promoting Native American philanthropy and increasing giving among Latinos are all important and necessary. Growing rural endowments is important, too. But none of these measures is sufficient to meet the needs of these communities.

It's time to get serious about asking and answering: *Who benefits from philanthropy?* This is a legitimate question raised with increasing frequency by the media and policy-makers. If foundation boards, however, don't wrestle with this question on their own and determine whether or not a sufficient percentage of their grant dollars are benefiting marginalized groups, then the Council on Foundations, affinity groups, the media and watchdog groups like my own, the National Committee for Responsive Philanthropy, should pressure foundation leaders to conduct that examination. Every foundation should be willing to ask whether their current grantmaking is doing enough to meet the needs of society while staying true to its mission. Many foundations ask these questions on a regular basis and are leaders in providing funding for rural communities or for other disadvantaged groups. But far too many foundations never ask the question in a serious way, and their peers let them get away with that lazy, comfortable approach to philanthropy.

...leaders in the philanthropic sector need to have the courage to make the case to their peers as to why foundations should be investing more in rural and other marginalized communities.

If we want to see real growth in rural philanthropy, we're going to have to convince some established foundations to recognize the potential positive impact that giving in rural America can have and to change their priorities. It's an argument that can be won on its own merits—no one needs to mandate from above more giving for rural communities—but leaders in the philanthropic sector need to have the courage to make the case to their peers as to why foundations should be investing more in rural and other marginalized communities.

No one can seriously argue that there isn't a problem with the lack of philanthropic dollars for rural America. A quick look at the numbers gives a snapshot of the disparity: In 2005, North Dakota nonprofits received the fewest grant dollars of any state—$8.8 million. In contrast, their New York counterparts received 254 times that and the most of any state—$2.24 billion.[1] When the dollar amounts are distributed across the number of grants given in each state, North Dakota averaged $40,000 per grant, compared with $135,000 in New York and $121,750 nationally. To break it down even further, the money amounts to $116 of grant funding per capita in New York and $13.80 per capita in North Dakota. Part of this stark difference can certainly be attributed to the difference in foundation presence in each state. In New York, 9,016 foundations held a total of $91.4 billion in assets in 2005; North Dakota's 80 foundations held just

[1] FC Stats: The Foundation Center's Statistical Information Service, "Geographic Distribution of Grants Awarded and Grants Received by State, circa 2005," http://foundationcenter.org/findfunders/statistics/pdf/03_fund_geo/2005/08_05.pdf The population of New York is about 30 times that of North Dakota.

over $193 million that same year.[2] However, just showing the need won't convince anyone to fund in rural communities who isn't already doing so.

Five Obstacles to Rural Grantmaking

Earlier this year, the National Committee for Responsive Philanthropy released a publication that helps explain the underlying real-world challenges behind these numbers. In the report *Rural Philanthropy: Building Dialogue from Within*, NCRP identifies five major obstacles to rural grantmaking and four strategies being employed to address those challenges.

The first obstacles deal with perceptions of rural life in America. In conversation after conversation, rural nonprofit leaders identified overly positive or overly negative perceptions as hindering access to foundation dollars. They lamented the "backwater" image that many Americans—including foundation staff—associate with rural America. This perception ranges from the romanticized and idyllic to the unsophisticated and uncultured. The former includes assumptions that rural communities are self-sufficient with little need for philanthropic dollars, while the latter conjures a less-than-attractive picture that turns off potential donors.

Our research also found that foundations perceive a lack of organizational capacity in rural nonprofits that translates into a bias when it comes to grantmaking. In evaluating potential grantees, foundations choose not to fund rural organizations due to a perception that they are lacking in a range of essential capacities, from leadership structure to staff specialization to financial controls. In many cases, the perceived lack of capacity is simply false—many rural nonprofits have greater competence than it appears. In other cases, the perceived lack of capacity is accurate, yet few foundations have been willing to invest in ways that will help rural nonprofits build their capabilities.

The third major obstacle faced by rural nonprofits is that they are disadvantaged when competing with organizations based in urban areas for foundation resources. Traditional foundation funding and program assessment relies heavily on a model that weighs impact by measuring the number of clients served. For foundations funding initiatives in rural areas, the quantitative return on investment makes such a venture appear undesirable. Many funders who have decided to fund in rural areas use different approaches for considering impact.

In a sector where fundraising and development relies heavily on cultivating relationships with funders, rural nonprofits are often isolated by distance from

[2]FC Stats: The Foundation Center's Statistical Information Service, "Fiscal Data of Grantmaking Foundations by State, circa 2005," http://foundationcenter.org/findfunders/statistics/pdf/01_found_fin_data/2005/01_05.pdf

major grantmaking institutions and lack the resources to attend conferences or other opportunities to meet with foundation staff. Unlike urban nonprofits, there are few opportunities to network locally.

Finally, rural nonprofits often do not have access to nonprofit professional associations, forums and events that their urban counterparts enjoy as an essential part of operation. This weak local infrastructure is a serious obstacle to grantmaking.

Four Strategies to Strengthen Rural Philanthropy

Understanding the challenges is important so that we can overcome them. NCRP's research identified four strategies to strengthen rural philanthropy and assessed the effectiveness of those strategies.

One strategy being used to strengthen rural grantmaking is the provision of multi-year general operating support. Rural nonprofits absolutely need this kind of long-term funding, which can be parlayed into a capacity-building tool. Multi-year flexible support with technical assistance allows rural organizations to increase staff, plan for the long term, and build institutional capacity. Foundations benefit from building and sustaining strong rural nonprofits that run successful programs and help transform communities.

Another popular strategy is to fund intermediaries. In the case of rural nonprofits, helpful types of intermediaries include regranters, capacity-building organizations or a combination of both. Our research found that this strategy comes with a few caveats: to be most effective, foundations need to choose the right intermediaries and should not forgo building a direct relationship with rural nonprofits. Intermediaries shouldn't substitute for direct exposure to foundations, especially considering this type of support tends to be episodic rather than long-term.

The establishment of collaboratives that draw new foundations in to rural grantmaking and build on the strengths of current funders is another strategy being employed. Funder collaboratives rely on pooled resources to achieve a greater impact on an issue area than any one single member could otherwise effect. In terms of rural philanthropy, funder collaboratives, whether regional or national in scale, represent an opportunity for rural areas to benefit from significant untapped philanthropic wealth. In 2002, two national funders—the W.K. Kellogg Foundation and the Ford Foundation—accounted for nearly half the total giving categorized as "rural development grants."[3] Clearly,

---

[3] FC Stats: The Foundation Center's Statistical Information Service, "Fiscal Data of Grantmaking Foundations by State, circa 2005," http://foundationcenter.org/findfunders/statistics/pdf/01_found_fin_data/2005/01_05.pdf

funder collaboratives diversify available funding, allow new foundations to explore rural philanthropic ventures and increase opportunities for rural nonprofits to access foundation dollars.

Finally, locally controlled funding streams are essential to the long-term viability of rural nonprofits. Local endowments engage communities, build a sense of ownership over the fundraising process and create money that is available to local-interest projects that would otherwise have difficulty winning dollars from national grant opportunities. Additionally, endowments are permanent, interest-generating funds with the potential to enhance rural nonprofit infrastructure and sustain programs in the long term. Our research found that while these developments are exciting for the future of funding for rural nonprofits, there is still a vast monetary divide that cannot wait for local endowment campaigns. Local endowments for rural communities are no substitute for immediate support from national and regional foundations.

But the most promising approach to increasing funding for rural America comes from Colorado, where the Anshutz Family Foundation has been leading Rural Philanthropy Days for the past 15 years. Their efforts have helped quintuple giving to rural parts of the state during that time period. In a disciplined and systematic approach, they engage politicians, foundations and nonprofit organizations in regular site visits throughout the state. The visits show how effective rural grantmaking can be and help build new relationships that often lead to funding. The Anshutz Family Foundation and their partners seek out new investors strategically. They are not afraid to suggest to a foundation that there is both a need and an opportunity in rural grantmaking.

So if we truly want to see real growth in grants to rural areas, we need to throw out the unwritten rule that says we can't suggest to other foundations what they should fund. We need courageous leaders who will ask their peers to examine their grantmaking priorities and find ways to include rural nonprofits in their giving portfolio.

Aaron Dorfman is Executive Director of the National Committee for Responsive Philanthropy, a national watchdog organization whose mission is to promote philanthropy that serves the public good, is responsive to people and communities with the least wealth and opportunity, and is held accountable to the highest standards of integrity and openness. A former community organizer, Dorfman studied political science and grassroots social movements at Carleton College under the direction of the late Senator Paul Wellstone and did his graduate work in philanthropic studies at Indiana University's Center on Philanthropy.

Michael Schechtman

"Stuck Situations" in the Philanthropic Divide: The Need for Nonprofit Capacity

U.S. Senate Finance Committee Chairman Max Baucus and the Council on Foundations have brought national attention and focus to the philanthropic challenges and long-term, systemic under-funding of rural America. The conference held in Missoula, Montana, in August, 2007, showcased excellent projects in rural America that have been supported by some of the most thoughtful foundations in the country. Field trips organized by the Montana Community Foundation exposed attendees to exciting programs and projects being conducted by terrific local nonprofits. Many attendees left the conference energized to learn more and possibly fund the vital new work they had seen; others talked about exploring with philanthropic colleagues whether these programs could be replicated in the rural areas tied to their mission's focus.

There was also genuine frustration among a number of conference attendees. Lurking in the wings was the crucial question: Why does so little foundation money make its way to rural America? On the first day of the conference, Aaron Dorfman, executive director of the National Committee for Responsive Philanthropy, highlighted findings from Rachael Swierzewski's report published by NCRP, *Rural Philanthropy: Building Dialogue From Within*. Dorfman noted that "inadequate organizational capacity" is one of the key barriers NCRP identified that constrains grants to rural nonprofits by regional and national foundations.

One of the sessions on the last day addressed how to build philanthropy for rural America, and much attention was given to the Intergenerational Transfer of Wealth. Participants pointed to the vital role that local community foundations can play in helping capture a portion of the wealth transfer as a community-focused philanthropic legacy for generations to come. Frustration surfaced once again, this time over the poignant reality that many areas in rural America lack adequate philanthropic infrastructure to engage and assist rural residents regarding the Transfer of Wealth and the possibility of leaving a philanthropic legacy.

Disparities in Funding for Rural and Urban Areas

Building institutional infrastructure in rural America that can guide and nurture the development of philanthropy and nonprofits is a core strategy for both building local philanthropy and attracting a more equitable share of the nation's annual foundation grantmaking. States vary with respect to their resources and capacity to build such infrastructure, which led my organization, the Montana-based Big Sky Institute for the Advancement of Nonprofits (BSI), to undertake research to document and articulate these disparities. BSI's findings documented long-term systemic under-funding of a number of low-population rural states, a phenomenon BSI refers to as the "Philanthropic Divide."

The Philanthropic Divide is a complex phenomenon of limited philanthropic and non-profit sector resources and infrastructure that places nonprofits in the 10 Divide states at a competitive disadvantage with their counterparts in other states. For most of the last 15 years, the 10 Philanthropic Divide states have been Alaska, Montana, Wyoming, North Dakota, South Dakota, Mississippi, West Virginia, New Hampshire, Vermont and Maine.[1] BSI has documented not only significant disparities in in-state foundation assets, but also in in-state per capita grantmaking. Limited foundation assets and low per capita grantmaking have been the lightning rod to draw attention to these states, whose operating conditions for nonprofits represent the extreme manifestation of the challenges and barriers facing rural America more generally.

In particular, the term "Philanthropic Divide" has been used to focus on the rapidly increasing gap in in-state foundation assets between those states with the least and those with the most. According to data published in 1990 by the Foundation Center, the 10 states with the least amount of foundation assets had an average of $63 million per state. The 10 states with the most assets had an average of almost $9.26 billion per state. The asset gap, comparing averages of the bottom 10 states with the top 10 states, was $9.2 billion. According to data published in 2007 by the Foundation Center, the average amount of assets among the bottom 10 states had increased to $757 million per state, while the top 10 states averaged $36.8 billion per state. The Philanthropic Divide asset gap had nearly *quadrupled* to $36.1 billion.

When BSI first published its data regarding the Philanthropic Divide, some foundation staff scoffed at the numbers, alleging that there were so few people in these states that very few assets were needed to satisfy the funding needs of these states' nonprofits.

---

[1] Data published in 2007 by the Foundation Center indicate that Wyoming and Maine have pushed their way out of the bottom ten, being replaced by New Mexico and Idaho. BSI is currently engaged in research activities that will develop a more comprehensive and definitive set of philanthropic metrics and associated indicators regarding Philanthropic Divide designation. It is anticipated that when the research is completed, the number of states receiving Philanthropic Divide designation will be greater than ten.

However, when BSI examined figures for per capita grantmaking among these states, we once again found significant disparities, which grew over time. Data published by the Foundation Center in 2007 pegged *per capita grantmaking* for the 10 states with the least assets at $34, compared to a national average of $117, and $171 per capita for the states with the most assets. Comparing averages among the bottom 10 states to the top 10 states showed a per capita grantmaking gap of $73 according to 2000 figures, with that gap increasing to $137 seven years later.

The paucity of foundation resources in the Philanthropic Divide states is critically important to the question of how infrastructure can be built to assist in the development of philanthropic and nonprofit capacity for these rural states. In Montana, for example, the great majority of the in-state foundations are small and unstaffed. Most grantmaking is at the $10,000 level or less. Relatively few grants are made in the $50,000 to $100,000 range, and grants over $100,000 are scarce at best. The building of nonprofit and philanthropic infrastructure has generally been the domain of foundations that can make large grants ranging from $100,000 to $250,000 and greater. This led BSI to examine grantmaking by the Top 50 Foundation Grantmakers to each of the 10 Divide states during the years 2000 through 2004. These preliminary findings were both illuminating and disturbing.

Grantmaking to the 10 Philanthropic Divide states by the 50 Top Foundation grantmakers (by giving) to each state increased from a total of $205.9 million in 2000 to $320.9 million in 2004. Most of this growth, however, came from in-state foundations. The in-state foundations that made the Top 50 in their respective states in 2000 granted a total of $22.5 million that year; this increased to $122.6 million in 2004. Top 50 grantmaking to the Divide states from national foundations was $103.7 million in 2000. By 2004, however, the national foundation total had declined to $96 million. More importantly, the percentage of total Top 50 grant dollars from national foundations to the Philanthropic Divide states declined precipitously from a very significant 50.4 percent in 2000 to 29.9 percent in 2004.

Work Underway to Build Infrastructure
to Strengthen Rural Philanthropy and Nonprofits

The Philanthropic Divide states have not sat by idly, awaiting a reversal in national foundation grantmaking trends, to figure out how to build infrastructure that can strengthen philanthropy and nonprofits. Some brief examples:

- In Alaska, nonprofit and philanthropic leaders worked together to found the Foraker Group, which is currently a multi-million dollar management support organization providing consulting, training and management support services to nonprofits of all sizes throughout this vast state with many remote and isolated communities.

- West Virginia established the West Virginia Grantmakers Association with a full-time Executive Director to serve and help strengthen the state's growing ranks of family foundations, as well as a consortium of 26 local community foundations.

- In New Hampshire, a consortium of in-state funders pooled resources to under-write a multi-year nonprofit capacity building initiative, in which the state's non-profit association, the New Hampshire Center for Nonprofits, has ramped up and emerged with an extremely robust program of professional development and Board training opportunities for nonprofits all over the state.

In Montana, special attention has been given to organizing and incubating diverse partnerships in order to coalesce resources and leadership to underwrite infrastructure development. Two illustrative examples are: the Montana Nonprofit Organizational Effectiveness Grantmaking Program and the Indian Philanthropy and Nonprofit Group Initiative.

BSI has partnered with a growing collaboration of in-state foundations to develop the Montana Nonprofit Organizational Effectiveness Grantmaking Program. Currently, if a nonprofit decides it wants to strengthen its capacity—whether it be through develop-ing a strategic plan, improving its financial management systems, diversifying its fund-ing or conducting board development activities—there are no statewide grantmaking programs to which nonprofits can turn for support to hire a consultant.

In addition to seed funding from the W.K. Kellogg Foundation for the OEG Program, seven Montana foundations have provided funds for this initiative, and several others are exploring participation this year. Program partners worked in collaboration with BSI and several national consultants to design the Montana OEG Program, which is

The Philanthropic Divide states have not sat by idly, awaiting a reversal in national foundation grantmaking trends, to figure out how to build infrastructure that can strengthen philanthropy and nonprofits.

being launched with a budget between $150,000 and $200,000. Following six months of program development work during the first half of 2008, the OEG Program will begin making grants for organizational assessments, as well as grants to support organizational development projects. Current plans call for three years of demonstration activities, followed by evaluation and assessment to determine how to continue the program on a sustainable basis.

Senator Baucus' interest in growing philanthropy for Montana and the rest of rural America is strongly mirrored by the interests of the state's governor, Brian Schweitzer. Governor Schweitzer hosted a Conversation on Endowments and Philanthropy in November of 2006 that generated keen interest in building philanthropy for Indian Country in Montana. Governor Schweitzer has appointed more Native Americans to his cabinet than any other governor in Montana's history. He supported his economic development specialist for the seven Indian reservations in Montana and the Coordinator of Indian Affairs to work with the Governor's Task Force on Endowments and Philanthropy and BSI to develop an initiative to build philanthropic resources and nonprofit development assistance for Indian-led nonprofits on the reservations and urban-based Indian communities. At present, this effort is known as the Indian Philanthropy and Nonprofit Group Initiative.

At its heart, the IPNG Initiative has brought together leadership from Indian Country, state government, in-state foundations and nonprofit sector infrastructure organizations to develop a long-term collaboration. A 24-member working group has begun sharing information to develop common understandings regarding nonprofit needs in Indian Country, the availability of resources within the state, new and emerging programs and projects that potentially could be tailored to assist nonprofits in Indian Country, and trends/new opportunities within regional and national funding circles. When this initial work to build shared understandings is completed, the working group will establish priorities and plans for building philanthropy and nonprofit resources for Indian Country. BSI is providing fiscal sponsorship, as well as incubation services, during this initial development stage.

In both of these examples, Montanans have taken "stuck situations" and created new strategies to get them "unstuck." All too often, infrastructure development in a Philanthropic Divide state like Montana has appeared far too daunting in complexity and cost for individual foundations to become involved. Historically, the localized focus of so many of the state's grantmakers, the lack of a statewide grantmakers association, and the overall problem of geographic isolation have constrained funders from getting their arms around these infrastructure development needs. Efforts by Philanthropy Northwest, the Governor's Task Force on Endowments and Philanthropy, the Montana Nonprofit Association, BSI and others have helped establish a new chapter in building diverse partnerships and better resourced collaborations. These promising efforts also present new opportunities for regional and national foundations to partner with in-state organizations where there is a confluence of interest in developing infrastructure that can help build philanthropy and nonprofit capacity.

Despite the overall positive tone and constructive direction of the rural philanthropy conference in Missoula, those of us living and working in rural states are still asking the important question: Why are so few national and regional foundation dollars making their way to rural areas? With promising and successful efforts like those described in this essay, and many more that also could be highlighted, rural and national foundations need to recognize that the old excuses are no longer valid. Terrific organizations doing fabulous work stand ready to partner with interested funders.

Michael Schechtman is Executive Director of Big Sky Institute for the Advancement of Nonprofits in Helena, Montana.

Karl Stauber

Rural America and Philanthropy: Challenges and Opportunities

It is a challenging time to be in philanthropy and in rural America. Both rural America and philanthropy are struggling to find new, more successful models—like many other segments of the U.S. "system." Everywhere one looks, you see organizations and sectors that are trying to find the "new" path. This is true of newspapers, hospitals, schools, financial institutions, cultural organizations, municipal governments, manufacturing firms and even the U.S. Army.

We think of rural America as a simpler place, with a slower pace. But from a public policy and community development perspective, those pre-conceptions are incorrect. Just as Charleston and Portland are very different, so is one rural community from another. In fact, the federal government has six different definitions of rural. For example, the Census Bureau defines rural as not urban based on population density, the Office of Management and Budget defines rural as not urban based on number of people in a city or county, and the Economic Research Service of the United States Department of Agriculture looks at degrees of rurality based on population, density and proximity to urban areas.

But one thing rural communities of various definitions and dimensions have in common: They are undergoing very rapid change. And much of it is not positive.

Rural America's Two Great Challenges

Much of rural America faces two great challenges—how to create a new economy, and how to create a new culture. Communities that can meet both challenges will prosper; those that meet only one will struggle; and those that do neither will die. These challenges are greater in areas where population is already declining and the economy already moribund. Rural areas that lack the three "Ts" suggested by noted author and academic Richard Florida—Talent, Technology and Tolerance—may be at greatest risk.

In many ways, these are the challenges facing all of America today. But in many rural areas these two great challenges are not something that *may* happen in a few years as the population ages, as more young people leave for a hotter lifestyle somewhere else, as poverty and social isolation become bigger issues, as health care and education become increasingly second class. All those challenges are happening in rural areas right now.

These challenges are complicated by the mythology of self-sufficiency in rural areas. In the West the mythology focuses on "making it on your own." In reality almost none of us live in self-sufficient communities. We buy cars from somewhere else, we use energy that almost always comes from somewhere else, we are cared for by medical personnel from somewhere else—maybe even another country, we attend schools built and staffed by someone else. Elsewhere, in the Midwest, East and South, the myth is more focused on "we take care of our own." But we almost never do. In these areas self-sufficiency often translates into low taxes, low services, low capacity and a culture of survival rather than prosperity.

Philanthropy's Shifting Focus

Right now is also a time of great challenge for organized philanthropy, especially nationally focused funders. Philanthropy should be about making change, not making grants. For much of the 20th century, the leading edge of philanthropy, especially national philanthropy, was identifying promising social innovations, evaluating them and then attempting to transfer them to the federal government. This produced innovations like Head Start, public television, educational equity for women and girls (Title IX) and even the painted lines on the sides of highways.

But this federally focused "theory of change" assumes that the government is expanding and it wants new challenges. The most successful recent national innovation that started with the help of philanthropy actually seems to be the opposite of what we have seen in the past. The charter school movement is at least in part about the perceived failure of publicly run K-12 education to serve children well. So philanthropy has created an innovation and then used the national government to help take authority and responsibility away from government. For some philanthropists the theory of change has become focused on diminishing governments' roles.

Regardless of your political ideology, we are facing a fundamental fiscal issue in the U.S. Even if we were to reverse all of President George W. Bush's tax cuts and exclude the debt from the current wars in South/Central Asia, the discretionary part of the U.S. budget will shrink for the next 20 years. As experts like Isabel Sawhill of the Brookings Institution suggest, we are facing huge challenges as our mandatory expenses (social security, Medicaid, Medicare) consume an increased percentage of the domestic budget, leaving less for discretionary spending and almost nothing for innovation.

New Behavior to Turn Challenges into Opportunities

So who will philanthropy sell our new ideas to if no one at the federal level is buying? Most foundations may be staffed by people who still see the "sell it to the feds" as the ideal. But communities that have decided to strive for more positive futures may be the next great audience for national foundations. National funders need new agents that can help take and return innovations to the local level, without depending on the national government as the primary means of diffusion.

While some see our rural areas as the backwater, they are actually at the leading edge for what may be the future of many communities. Rural areas represent a great opportunity for philanthropy to learn about community transformation—before the potential cultural and economic crises get to the affluent but more challenging urban regions.

Yet rural America and philanthropy are words and worlds that rarely intersect. Most foundations and corporate giving programs are urban-based. And most charitable giving occurs close to home. There are important exceptions to these patterns when companies have major rural components (for example, the wood products industry), or when family foundations have rural areas as part of their family geography, or when independent and community foundations see rural as part of their area of interest. Then there are the small number of community and private foundations that are actually rural-based. But even with these exceptions, rural philanthropy is a very minor part of the field.

Dilemmas to Getting More Resources for Rural Needs

Those of us that live and work in rural areas would like to see more resources flowing this way. However, to move more resources to rural we are faced with two dilemmas— a double-yoked "chicken or egg."

First Dilemma—The Zero Sum Challenge. Put simply, if rural areas are going to get more philanthropic resources, who will get less? In almost every issue of the *Chronicle of Philanthropy* there is a good argument for putting more money into X—health care for the poor, art museums, community capacity development, nuclear disarmament, immigration reform; the list is nearly infinite. With demand nearly infinite and supply clearly finite, there is an imbalance. For every Member of Congress that says spend more on rural, there are approximately nine who may say no (of the 435 Representatives, only around 45 come from districts that the United States Department of Agriculture identifies as primarily rural). And in reality, just as rural areas get a small proportion of philanthropic resources, they get a small proportion of the federal budget.

In some parts of the country, rural communities are addressing this dilemma directly by focusing on wealth-capturing strategies, often led by community foundations. One sees this "Grow Your Own" strategy in a variety of rural settings from New Hampshire to Nebraska to California. The GYO strategy has great potential over the long term, but its impact on current challenges is limited and it does not work in the poorest parts of rural America. If you don't have wealth to capture, wealth-capturing obviously will not work.

Second Dilemma—Capacity Begets Resources. Low-capacity communities (urban and rural) are at a significant disadvantage when it comes to competing for philanthropic (or government) resources. Disconnected people and communities never see a "level playing field"; they may never see any field. Often, the more isolated and under capacity a community is, the less likely it is to even know about foundations, much less compete successfully for resources.

Over the last three decades there have been numerous efforts to build community capacity—Ford Foundation's efforts to nurture rural community development corporations; targeted regional efforts by many funders like the Charles Stewart Mott, W.K. Kellogg and Northwest Area Foundations, the New Hampshire Community Trust, and the Duke and California Endowments, to mention just a few; and rural leadership development efforts by funders including the Blandin and Ford Family Foundations and the Foundation for the Mid South. But such efforts are often hard to sustain over time and it can be difficult to demonstrate impact. Like other rural-focused efforts, these can unintentionally turn into ways of exporting some of the most talented people from rural communities.

Intermediaries as the Missing Link?

The missing link in this new opportunity may be regional intermediaries. National funders rarely have the ability to reach down to the community level. Rural nonprofits rarely know how to meaningfully engage national funders. Historically, regional intermediaries have played a bridging role. Sometimes these are based in community foundations, such as the Humboldt Area Foundation in California; sometimes they are nationally specialized nonprofits, such as the Center for Community Change, North Carolina's MDC and the First Nations Development Institute; or blended organizations such as the Minnesota Initiative Foundations created by the McKnight Foundation.

There is a great opportunity for national and multi-state regional funders to come together and identify rural areas where there are real opportunities to explore the creation of new cultures and new economies, even as these same regions are clear about what part of their old cultures and economies they wish to sustain. If national funders could develop such "regions of opportunity" and invite local organizations to organize such intermediaries, the United States would once again be creating a new "theory of change," one that is not dependent on the national government, but one that does see the feds as a partner. If national funders were to undertake such an approach, it would require of rural groups their own version of cooperation that has often been absent in the past. Rural organizations would have to undergo their own cultural shift, acknowledging that "together has more potential than apart." If the rural groups do not take such a position, the efforts of the national funders to work with intermediaries are likely to be unsuccessful.

Rural America—you can look at it as a place that reflects our past or as a place that foretells our future. It is one of the first parts of America to engage the challenges of creating a new economy and a new culture. Support from national and urban funders can help insure the success of rural regions and serve as a model of successful transformation. Without that success, what is the future any of us have to look forward to?

Karl Stauber is President & CEO of the Danville Regional Foundation, serving parts of Southside Virginia and adjacent North Carolina. Prior to joining DRF in August 2007, Stauber served in a similar capacity at the Northwest Area Foundation based in Minnesota for eleven years. He was an under secretary at USDA in the Clinton Administration and has worked on issues related to rural development and philanthropy for over 30 years.

Partnerships and Changing How People Think

"Hard to reach." That's an interesting choice of words I heard someone recently use to describe the Mid South's rural areas. The Mid South —Arkansas, Louisiana and Mississippi—possesses large, open areas of farmland that, at one time, helped to make cotton king and placed our three states among the most vibrant and economically flush in the nation. After the Civil War, our region's economy and population changed significantly and it still struggles to find a competitive advantage in the nation's and world's economy. Despite the creativity, resilience and resourcefulness of its people, the Mid South currently ranks among the poorest, unhealthiest and least educationally competitive states in the nation.

Interestingly, the phrase does not clarify whether "hard to reach" describes the geographic location or the receptiveness of local residents to outside interests, ideas and assistance. This is particularly relevant when one recognizes that in some areas of the Mid South, there are small, unincorporated communities comprised of eighth generation families—and they *ain't* going anywhere, or changing their tune, anytime soon. The history of these communities and their leadership directly affects their ability to create an atmosphere that supports the creation of new, diverse and inclusive partnerships and ideas to tackle their community's most significant barriers to progress.

What Does *Rural* Mean?

Merriam-Webster defines *rural* as "open land, relating to country, country people or life, or agriculture." To add further clarity, organizations like the U.S. Census Bureau, the Office of Management and Budget and the Economic Research Service of the United States Department of Agriculture have defined rural areas through quantifiable criteria and labels for the various stages of community development, based upon an area's population, workforce or geography.

While I'm sure these labels are helpful to government officials and scholars, the reality is that the concept of rural is as diverse as the landscape of our nation. Understandably, it is difficult to grasp the various aspects of what constitutes a "rural" area. In line with most definitions, rural can describe small, agricultural communities. Rural in other areas can be classified as a geographically isolated community or one that does not have a strong economic driver to boost the local economy. One test does work particularly well when determining whether an area is rural or not: Ask the locals—they'll tell you the correct answer.

In the Mid South, our experience with the concept of rural encompasses much of what most—I believe—would consider rural. In the Delta region of Arkansas, Louisiana and Mississippi, we have many sparsely populated communities, unincorporated towns and economies driven predominantly by agriculture. But just as the tapestry of rural areas nationally is varied, the Mid South is quite varied, too. For instance, many communities, such as those in the Mississippi Gulf Coast, might not be viewed as rural in the traditional sense, but many of these communities still meet the criteria in population size and economies. Other areas, such as east Mississippi and west Arkansas, also consist of small, unincorporated hamlets but are home to either an anchor industry (like Wal-Mart in northwest Arkansas) or universities (like Mississippi State University and the University of Mississippi in northeast Mississippi).

Also, the changing landscape and environment of the Mid South plays an integral role in the formation and sustainability of communities. The Delta possesses some of the best farmland in the nation because of the richness of the soil that is deposited by the Mississippi River. But pollution and other environmental conditions over the years (some of which our area has inherited from the North) are affecting the agriculture and fishing industries in our region. Another Mid South area, South Louisiana, boasts many economic assets that range from sugar cane to coffee to oil and natural gas, but this part of the state is dotted with very small communities due, in part, to the geography along the Gulf in Louisiana that makes it difficult to develop because of the wetlands and its propensity to flood.

Context Matters

In the deep South, when one requests a soft drink—regardless the flavor or manufacturer—it is oftentimes referred to as "a Coke." When the beverage arrives, two outcomes can be expected: Either an actual Coca-Cola is delivered, or the soda provider brings the requestor her known favorite soda, which very well may not be a Coke.

While my soda anecdote does not have much to do with how partnerships occur in rural communities, it does illustrate how even specific terms like Coke can be subjective and can mean different things to different people based upon their experiences and views. The diversity in the understanding of "rural" makes this term extremely subjective.

For example, a person's description of his *rural* summer ranch out West can convey a significantly different image and connotation from that of a person who lives in the Mid South—especially those from or with knowledge of the Delta region of Arkansas, Louisiana and Mississippi. If a Mid South Delta resident were asked to define or explain the concept of rural, more than likely she would include the descriptor "poor" somewhere in the answer.

In understanding and discussing "rural" areas, context definitely matters. And in these conversations, it is important to acknowledge and accept that experience and geography will influence the topics, priorities, politics and even the passion of discussions centered on rural areas.

The Challenges in the Rural Mid South

Over the past forty years, local and national donors and foundations have invested significantly in the Delta regions of Arkansas, Louisiana and Mississippi. Among those that have exhibited a commitment to the region's progress have been the Walton Family Foundation, Ford Foundation, W.K. Kellogg Foundation, Margarite Casey Foundation, and the Mary Reynolds Babcock Foundation, to name a few.

This speaks volumes to the lure of the Delta. The Delta continues to be the philan-thropic big fish that eludes capture, in the sense that it possesses one of the highest concentrations of poverty in the nation; it lacks—due to the persistent poverty of its residents—the robust tax base necessary to adequately fund and improve physical infrastructure and local schools; it possesses a relatively unskilled, uneducated work-force; and it has a notorious history of racial, social and economic disparity.

The Delta has been the focus for many organizations seeking to reduce poverty and to improve health, education and racial reconciliation, among other issues. While many of these groups have made progress in their endeavors, the Delta has not undergone the renaissance that is longed for. The big fish and the solutions to cure the region's woes continue to elude its captors. With so much in the way of resources and human capital working in the Delta, how have thoughtful and effective solutions to its problems not been found and implemented in this region? How does the fish keep getting away?

Donors and foundations who wish to work in the rural areas of the Mid South should make a conscious and thoughtful decision to be open to developing and adopting new strategies for how they will partner in the region. To truly meet the needs of individuals and communities, partnerships must be created that are inclusive, adaptable, diverse, trusting and open to new ideas.

> With so much in the way of resources and human capital working in the Delta, how have thoughtful and effective solutions to its problems not been found and implemented in this region? How does the fish keep getting away?

Can "Partnerships" Truly Exist in the Mid South?

Sectoral groups working in isolation on the priority issues they alone have identified are missing an opportunity to effect widespread change at the community level. Essentially, they are providing short-term solutions to remedy specific problems, but they are unable to provide the solutions that either eliminate the root cause of persistent disparities or that benefit all people in a community.

Historically speaking, many efforts in the Delta have been managed this way: Donors or organizations have created hypotheses and worked to prove the effectiveness of their ideas in a rural area in the Mid South. Sometimes, they were successful. But oftentimes, the work was conducted strictly on the experimenter's terms and excluded or alienated sectors of the community. Upon evaluation, the unsuccessful efforts tended to point to the negatives they faced: the overwhelming need, inadequate time or funding, or the lack of widespread participation or "buy in" from the community. On the other hand, we noticed that the successful efforts reflected on positives: the creativity and resourcefulness of the people, the assets a community already possesses, and the development of effective solutions based on the input of the people most affected.

In recent years, there seems to be an awareness of the importance of partnerships in efforts to improve the region. Foundations are collaborating in greater numbers and local communities are increasingly becoming part of the change that they wish to see. Many efforts are finding success due in part to this "buy in" from the local community.

While some strides are being made on the partnership front—particularly along the Gulf Coast, severely impacted by Hurricanes Katrina and Rita—there are still areas where improvement can be made. Those wishing to affect positive change in rural areas and seeking partnerships to do so must incorporate a holistic approach. A single, thoughtful group of like-minded folks led by a foundation or other community-based organization can make huge contributions to improving communities. But without the inclusion of those in traditional leadership positions, in business, coupled with the vision, experience and support of local residents, these efforts will not ultimately result in solutions that are deep and wide and helpful to those most affected.

In many situations, only those who already possess the skills and competencies to become effective leaders receive the opportunities to expand their talents and serve their communities. With our region's widespread poverty and lack of human resources, the progress of our region relies heavily on identifying and building new leadership from all segments of our population. In our rural communities, attention should be focused on increasing the capacity and expanding the vision of the local, indigenous populations.

One of our region's most critical challenges to overcome in both our rural and urban areas is to change the way people think. How can leaders accept and influence others to believe in the concept that poverty and a lack of inclusion diminishes the quality of life for *all* people—not just those of few or no resources and the disenfranchised? Instead of protecting what they consider *theirs*, how can we get our residents, civic leaders, business leaders and nonprofit leaders to work together in greater numbers toward their common goals? If these efforts to form symbiotic partnerships fail to occur naturally, how can they be facilitated in thoughtful ways that are inclusive in participation and decision making? The absence of these partnerships or of leadership's reluctance to be inclusive will only compromise the integrity of the community good and greatly reduce the potential of these communities to rise from poverty to prosperity.

Despite its many challenges, the rural Mid South possesses many significant assets, strengths and opportunities. A critical step in formalizing partnerships and identifying goals is simply to take time to identify and better understand what a community already has to build upon. It could be a robust local school system that could be marketed to attract new industry. It could be strong and diverse leadership in the different sectors within a community that could help catalyze and endorse community improvement efforts. It could be rich and fertile land that could interest new, innovative industries to establish their bases of operations. Regardless of the carrot that is used, the stick ultimately comes down to creating real, effective and diverse partnerships; working toward common goals; and, although they may receive support from outside sources, seeking long-term change that will improve *their* own communities.

Ivye L. Allen is President of the Foundation for the Mid South.

rural america tomorrow —
learning from philanthropy

philanthropy

&

rural america

section II

There is much philanthropy can do to help rural America adapt for the future. And many philanthropists and foundations are already learning what it takes to make an impact in rural areas. Essays in the following four chapters share some key insights and specific recommendations from philanthropy's work to date in helping rural America.

From the rise of rural development philanthropy to efforts at improving rural economics, education, environment and health, the assembled authors are experts on what philanthropy is doing, or should be doing, today for rural America tomorrow. Collectively, the authors report that success builds from persistence and perseverance—what Brad Crabtree calls foundations'"patient capital." It also requires risk-taking, collaboration and the direct involvement of a wide swath of the community, including both those young and old, the powerful and the disadvantaged or previously disengaged, and supporters *and* critics of community change.

An area's future is best shaped when it's in the hands of the people living and working there. But philanthropy can and should help point the way forward.

CHAPTER 3 |

The New
Rural Community

The New Realities of Rural America

*"It is increasingly clear that not only are the fates of rural
and urban people and places linked, but that these links grow
stronger as globalization, de-industrialization, suburbanization
and climate change accelerate. They provide an entry point for
creative new strategies regarding jobs, education, health, the
environment, race/ethnicity, political representation and the
values of community that cross political boundaries, value
systems and economic theories"*

> — Our Shared Fate: Bridging the Rural-Urban Divide
>   by the Roundtable on Community Change and
>   Community Strategies Group, The Aspen Institute

We as a country continue to look to the past, sometimes in reverence,
to our rural communities; to a time and place of seeming simplicity
compared to today when all the rules seem to be changing with
whirlwind speed. Yet the truth of rural life has veered dramatically
away from our nation's antiquated perceptions, and the immediate
trend lines to a shared future are intertwined with the new realities
of rural America.

Today, "urban" Americans can live in small towns or
the countryside without forgoing their professions. The
intersection of urban and rural interests is both politically
dynamic and dictated by self-interest: Rural America has
skills needed by all Americans as tenders of our small
towns, countryside and the environment; the health of
rural America and all Americans in the face of scarce
resources is intimately linked; and high-speed Internet
removes the distance from educational opportunity and
from many marketplaces.

> Philanthropy has an urgent and
> increasing role to play in helping us
> as a nation reframe our understanding
> of the interconnectedness of all our
> communities and the need to shift from
> silos of inquiry and response to systems
> of analysis and leverage.

The potential for improved life in our countryside, in
small towns and at their urban intersections should provide hope for
the future of all Americans. Philanthropy has an urgent and increasing
role to play in helping us as a nation reframe our understanding of the
interconnectedness of all our communities and the need to shift from

silos of inquiry and response to systems of analysis and leverage. The biggest barrier to community-friendly development is often outdated political jurisdictions, the subject of the growing regionalism movement. In the fluidity of foundation practices and boundaries communities can find ways to cross those barriers without waiting for the glacial pace of reform.

The gap between American's perceptions of rural life and the truth is well documented by the Center for Rural Strategies and through research commissioned by the W.K. Kellogg Foundation. Americans still picture rural residents primarily as part of the agricultural economy, white folks on tractors growing our nation's crops in the communities of their grandparents. The truth of today, in which only about 4 percent of people who live in the country are tied to the farm economy, is far more dynamic and diverse, and the rate of change increasing. The people least served by our nation's prosperity are of color *and* of rural communities.

Meanwhile, global, national and regional dynamics are changing the outlook for rural communities in America at a rate unprecedented in at least the last hundred years. Four vortexes are driving change: economic restructuring, environmental degradation, population growth and migration, and digital communication. While these forces are affecting virtually all of humanity, there are particular challenges and opportunities being created in America's small towns and countryside. Community foundations, in particular, are proving to have a powerful role to play:

> *"Community foundations are not inoculations against unforeseen change and unexpected cataclysm, but at their best they are measured, democratic practices that can marshal community aspiration and invigorate meaningful cooperation. And when that happens resources and opportunities seem to follow even in the poorest communities—sometimes when the outlook is bleakest. Neighbors become donors and give themselves a fighting chance for a decent future."*
>
> — Dee Davis, president of the Center for Rural Strategies,
>   from *Donors Ourselves*

The Rise in Rural Development Philanthropy

The rise of Rural Development Philanthropy (RDP) is helping advance community philanthropy as an effective tool in meeting the challenges of rural development. RDP began as peer learning funded by the Ford Foundation and convened by the Aspen Institute Community Strategies Group in 1991, and continues independently as a growing field of practice. RDP practitioners believe that success must be measured by the accomplishment of tangible systems improvement in specific communities, not by the aggregation of funds or the giving of grants, although these are among important supporting measurements.

For example, East Tennessee's Coker Creek and Greeneville are among many well-documented examples of RDP at work. Both Coker Creek and Greeneville were isolated and ravaged by the decline of the resource economy, and both worked over many years with the East Tennessee Foundation to build an economy and rebuild a dilapidated infrastructure around the skills, knowledge and industry of its residents based on a strong sense of place.

Though a survey is needed so that we know the full extent of RDP examples, other examples include: The Kenya Community Development Foundation has organized villagers to prioritize and organize efforts—as a result, a new network of reservoirs now guarantees water for crops; the Vermont Community Foundation uses its investment portfolio to provide loans to low-income people; and the Seventh Generation Fund has helped Native communities across the country develop sustainable agriculture. My own foundation, the Humboldt Area Foundation, has been a catalyst for regional agencies and community-based leaders to successfully rebuild the economies in our most central small towns after the catastrophic decline of the timber industry. We are now working to spread the benefits throughout the region.

Need for More Foundation Help in Meeting Rural Challenges

The long-term decline of farm, timber and other resource-based rural economies, for decades the root of an ongoing rural depression in many parts of the country, is giving way to a new era of entrepreneurship. Theories of economic and community development, nurtured and tested by such places as the RUPRI Center for Rural Entrepreneurship in Lincoln, Nebraska, are demonstrating that rural economies can thrive, and increasingly are thriving, based on the capacity of rural people to both civically engage and grow small business and diversified economies. Private foundations such as Kellogg have supported the work of the Center for Rural Entrepreneurship and community foundations such as the Nebraska Community Foundation and Humboldt Area Foundation have leveraged this investment with measurable and significant success.

Rural America is forging ahead with new solutions, and private foundations are playing an unusually important role in what proves to be fertile ground for innovation. A few areas of notable progress in improving rural America include: improving services to rural families (Annie E. Casey Foundation), developing combined economic and environmental rural development strategies (Kellogg and Ford Foundations), improving conditions for farm workers (The California Endowment), exploring models of new rural leadership (Oregon's Ford Family Foundation) and supporting essential university research (the California Endowment and the Kellogg, Casey and Ford Foundations). The knowledge and examples provided by these foundations are being adapted by rural community philanthropies, service agencies and other rural activists and advocates.

National and regional foundations should be linking with local philanthropy-based initiatives to help them expand rapidly to meet several major challenges, such as immigration and the environment. The opportunities are immediate and the fruit low-hanging for those community philanthropies that are prepared to act as brokers of knowledge and relationships, and to serve as a voice for vibrant democratic action and, when necessary, against stereotypes and racism.

The flood of immigrants to this country has shifted destination significantly from cities to rural areas, heretofore rarely directly affected since the large migrations of the 19th century. The rate of rural demographic change now often exceeds that of urban America. This is altering the politics of the entire country and is testing our tolerance as a "nation of nations," as Herman Melville wrote, as communities with no experience with large cultural and racial change are abruptly transformed. There is little evidence of action by community foundations in the more volatile regions where demographic change is new and sudden and the need for sound community-building competencies is the greatest.

As normal cycles of drought collide with population increase, areas of the nation, such as the Southeast, which have never before worried about water shortages, are suddenly in crisis. The need to plan and act systemically about the use of water (and by extension other resources) by cities, small towns and the countryside is inescapable. Atlanta realized this too late to avoid the outcomes of its recent drought, the answers to which lay far outside its borders in a four-state region. The El Paso Community Foundation could serve as a model for others to emulate in this regard. It has a distinguished history of mobilizing community response to water shortage in the Rio Grande valley (as well as working with new immigrant communities).

Some of America is at least temporarily losing population, a trend that is apt to reverse in many places where the cost of living is low, and where a diversified job base is only now becoming a potential as broadband Internet expands and makes working location flexible as never before. Many of these communities are held with passionate regard by those who live there. Nebraska, for example, the country of Willa Cather, recently spawned a movement for "HomeTown Competitiveness," as Jeff Yost details in his essay in this journal.

Other places in America are facing continued population expansion despite frustrated efforts to contain sprawl, and they are now realizing that small towns and places where almost no one may currently live are the population centers of tomorrow. If infrastructure—roads, electricity, water and high-speed Internet—are systemically developed and watersheds, protection of forest lands for jobs and for carbon sequestration, and clearing of forest under-story for wildfire mitigation are addressed, a new balance may be found for our growing nation. The Humboldt Area Foundation is working with Redwood Coast Rural Action, an inclusive regional leadership initiative, and the California Center for Rural Policy at Humboldt State University to help Sacramento build partnerships and networks with many types of organizations throughout the state.

The Need to Support and Spread Innovations

The dominant political power in most of America is now held by suburbs and exurbs, and conditions in both our small towns and large cities are often similar in educational outcomes, the building of infrastructure and environmental health. There is little political ability to make improvements unless urban and rural common cause can be reached. The role for rural and urban community philanthropy to bridge the gaps between urban and rural interests is ripe for action. Foundations not bound by jurisdictional lines have a critical role to play in building common cause across boundaries not well served by our political system.

The call to build a new consensus around federal rural policy may perhaps only be possible through the active combined engagement of large national or regional foundations, as well as those small and place-based. The fact that the Farm Bill represents too big of a plate of pork to attack directly does not mean that it is moral or palatable to let it obstruct a long overdue overhaul of rural policy and investments in rural America. As stated by Mark Drabenstott in the March 2005 *Main Street Economist*, a publication of the Federal Reserve Bank of Kansas City: "Farm payments are not providing a strong boost to the rural economy in those counties that most depend on them. Job gains are weak and population growth is actually negative in most of the counties where farm payments are the biggest share of income."

Despite startling inattention, rural America is a hotbed of innovation and growing experience with an emerging economy, effective entrepreneurship and environmental action. Many of our country's largest risks, such as global warming, the water crisis and urban sprawl, can only be remediated through active partnerships that authentically include, and are sometimes led by, residents in America's small towns and countryside.

Those working in community philanthropy, and indeed philanthropy in general, must move fast to help support and spread rural innovations underway, much less attend to the many unprecedented opportunities sweeping around us. We need more private foundations and community foundations stepping out of self-imposed silos to link the regions, issues and collaborative solutions to many of our nation's greatest challenges.

Peter Pennekamp is the Executive Director of California's Humboldt Area Foundation. He is an advocate for rural communities at the state and national levels and an activist for inclusive practices in our institutions and communities. Prior positions include vice president of National Public Radio and as a program director with the National Endowment for the Arts, both in Washington D.C.

Towards a More Democratic
Vision of Rural Community Giving

How ironic that America's most benevolent sector, philanthropy (philo + anthropos: "love of humankind"), is too often viewed as its most guarded, nurtured by the belief that true philanthropy—or "charity" as it has come to be seen—is the privilege and even the responsibility of the very wealthy to care for those less fortunate. Not to disparage the great, good things that philanthropy so conceived has been able to accomplish. But there is another, more democratic understanding of philanthropy gaining favor as a popular institution to benefit communities, wealthy and poor alike. This more common and participatory understanding of philanthropy can be characterized as "community philanthropy," with rural families and communities leading the way.

James Richardson

The National Rural Funders Collaborative (NRFC) was launched in the summer of 2001 as a philanthropic initiative of large national and regional funders,[1] initially motivated by the glaring imbalance between urban and rural philanthropic contributions and the intent of NRFC funders to learn how to make more effective rural investments. The intent of NRFC founders was to leverage $100 million in a 10-year period to support work in rural regions and to identify lessons that could inform other regional and national grantmakers.

Athan Lindsay

After awarding $3,071,760 in single and multiple-year grants from 2001 through 2005,[2] NRFC's member foundations and participating grantees worked together to reevaluate its mission and strategies for community transformation and to assess how the initiative could have greater impact and build more momentum for transforming rural communities and moving rural families out of poverty. With the help

---

[1] Original NRFC funders included the Mary Reynolds Babcock Foundation, Calvert Social Investment Foundation, Annie E. Casey Foundation, Fannie Mae Foundation, Ford Foundation, F.B. Heron Foundation, William Randolph Hearst Foundation, William and Flora Hewlett Foundation and W.K. Kellogg Foundation. Since then Bank of America Foundation, Otto Bremer Foundation, California Endowment, Lumina Foundation for Education and Northwest Area Foundation have also joined NRFC's membership.

[2] In the first phase of its work, NRFC made grants ranging from $50,000 to $750,000 to 17 diverse initiatives in 15 states and regions, thereby leveraging an additional $41 million in public and private sector funding. For more information on its first phase of funding, see *Transforming Rural America: Many Faces, Diverse Voices, Distant Places, Common Choices; Reflections from the first three years: 2002-2005 National Rural Funders Collaborative* at http://www.nrfc.org/nrfc/documents/nrfc.3yearreport.final.pdf .

of outside research and evaluation of its own work,[3] NRFC members recognized the full significance of the increasing diversity of rural communities and the importance of understanding the intersection of race, class, culture and power for addressing poverty in rural regions. The conclusion of that research was that NRFC's theory of change indicators—wealth creation, family self-sufficiency and civic participation/leadership—did not go far enough. While wealth creation, family self-sufficiency and civic participation/leadership transformation are indicative of poverty alleviation, these outcomes cannot be achieved without an analysis of and response to issues of race, class, culture and power, because rural poverty is "colorized."

Hence, NRFC's own final analysis of its work-to-date suggested several compelling conclusions:

- **Rural America is already being transformed.** Rural communities are being transformed by both dramatic demographic and economic changes that are adversely affecting people of color.

- **People of color who reside in rural America are disproportionately living in extreme poverty and persistently poor counties.** While combined communities of color only account for 17 percent of the total rural population, they are poor at two to three times the rate of their white counterparts. The "coloring of rural poverty" is demonstrated by glaring wage, health and educational disparities among people of color in rural regions.

- **The real causes of rural poverty are integrally linked to changes in the rural economy, particularly changes in the kinds of employment.** The lack of diversification, the growth of "big box retailers," prisons, and high-risk, low-wage, non-union retail, meat-packing and poultry industry jobs are converging to create an economy that keeps people poor. Because rural areas tend to have higher rates of underemployment and fewer community resources, when rural workers do find work, they are more likely to be employed and still poor.

These findings suggest that the reinvention of rural economies—ones with living wages, career-ladder employment and jobs that respect the environment and the health and safety of employees—is fundamental to addressing extreme and persistent rural poverty and forging positive transformative change in rural America. NRFC understands that poverty is often a factor of race, class, culture and power dynamics that are linked and concentrated.

---

[3]See *"Zeroing In: Choices and Challenges for the National Rural Funders Collaborative,"* Applied Research Center: Oakland, CA, July 2005 at http://www.nrfc.org/redesign/Zeroing_In-Fin2.pdf

Efforts aimed at poverty alleviation and wealth creation must first recognize that the work of building rural economies also entails confronting the structural barriers that foster racial disparities and discriminatory practices. Transforming extreme and persistently poor rural communities and regions into healthy and viable living environments will ultimately require the creation of a rural movement for social and economic equity—a convergence of grassroots efforts to envision, develop, implement and monitor a policy context grounded in the newly emerging realities of rural life.

With this revised sense of its mission, theory of change and way of working in hand, NRFC launched its new phase of work in 2006. Among new and revised set of underlying assumptions:

- Strong regional economies are essential to the success and well-being of local communities and families;

- Cultural and land-based economic development ventures and strategies offer significant opportunity to create healthy local and regional economies;

- Developing grassroots efforts to shape and develop the vision and change agenda is an essential aspect of growing local rural economies;

- The ability of rural community groups to identify and develop appropriate strategies to address race, class and power are key to the success of their efforts to transform their economies;

- New philanthropic models of "civic participation" and engagement must be developed to support these alternative, community asset-based rural economies.

This revised understanding of rural community transformation as a strategy for alleviating rural poverty has as its foundation stone the awareness that philanthropy as traditionally conceived may in reality be able to accomplish very little in this effort unless it first recognizes that this transformation must begin from within those communities themselves. This recognition sets the stage for understanding the importance of growing rural philanthropy as a broadly democratic and civic endeavor by means of which rural families—including a growing number of rural families of color—must design their own community-based strategies, models and institutions of support as a necessary preamble to asking philanthropy to join as a partner in supporting their efforts.

Philanthropy as an Opportunity for Civic Engagement

Consequently, the recognition that persistently poor regions too often have too little organized philanthropy or access to other forms of investment with which to sustain transformative work that builds alternative rural economies implies much more than a need for large national and regional philanthropies to step in and make more grants to rural regions. Additionally, and more importantly, it calls for the creation of new and alternative forms of philanthropy and other forms of community investment in which ordinary people and marginalized groups who live and work in rural communities can participate. In its most inclusive sense, philanthropy begins locally and is understood as civic participation in which all can help to shape their community's future.

This understanding of philanthropy as an opportunity for broad civic engagement in supporting community and its transformation has many new and emerging faces, but in actuality is very old and rooted in the many cultures and traditions found in rural areas in this country and others. Former Council on Foundations President and Ambassador to South Africa James A. Joseph published original research nearly two decades ago documenting the many indigenous giving traditions of cultures and communities of color as broad asset-based strategies for building and sustaining community.[4] This broader understanding of philanthropy as community philanthropy must include those who live and work in rural communities as part of the solution and not simply as the recipients of benevolent gifts. If strategies to address root causes of problems and to move those on the margins of our communities toward the mainstream are to be effective, individuals and communities must be included in their own development. Philanthropy viewed as community philanthropy should be seen as something which joins traditional philanthropic institutions and communities together in collective or collaborative strategies for community change.

> Community philanthropy recognizes that solutions to community problems often come from unexpected places and from people excluded from community decision making. When we look for models of community philanthropy, a strong argument can be made that rural communities and communities of color are leading the way.

Community philanthropy invests in and celebrates human competencies and cultural traditions as assets, and uses these resources to foster risk-taking and creativity in tackling community problems. Community philanthropy recognizes that solutions to community

---

[4]James A. Joseph. *The Charitable Impulse: Wealth and Social Conscience in Communities and Cultures Outside the U.S.* The Foundation Center. 1989.

problems often come from unexpected places and from people excluded from community decision making. When we look for models of community philanthropy, a strong argument can be made that rural communities and communities of color are leading the way.

Within African-American communities in the American South, there is an old and rich tradition of "giving" circles as a way for members of the community to pool their resources and invest in alternative futures for themselves and their neighbors. Giving circles build on the tradition of neighbor helping neighbor, collectively maximizing their 'time, talent and treasures' through civic engagement as well as financial contributions. Helping to foster and develop this tradition as a national, community-based movement has been Darryl Lester with Hindsight Consulting, which now supports an ongoing network and annual conference of giving circles known as the "Community Investment Network."[5]

This democratized or broad understanding of philanthropy can also be seen as a long-standing tradition finding new incarnations in Native American communities. As just one example of the use of giving circles and community philanthropy within Native American communities, Carrie Day Aspinwall, formerly the membership and program coordinator for Native Americans in Philanthropy, helped to develop NAP's Circle of Leadership. This program helps identify and teach young Native American leaders and expose them to the field of philanthropy, with hopes that they would take those skills back and implement philanthropic strategies in their own communities.[6]

These indigenous traditions for community philanthropy are not restricted to cultures and communities we think of as long-term residents within American society. In communities of Latino workers moving into rural America from Mexico and Central and South America, residents from common small towns of origin "across the border" are forming "hometown associations." These associations send remittances back to family and friends to support the struggling family and community economies back home. At the same time, these hometown associations are increasingly becoming the vehicle by means of which immigrants settling into American communities and regions as semi-permanent, if not permanent, residents are setting aside and pooling resources to support the livelihood and culture of friends and family in this country as well.

[5]See Community Investment Network: http://www.thecommunityinvestment.org/
[6]See http://www.nrfc.org/documents/Comm_Based_Philanthropy.pdf

Other models are arising within rural communities and regions, many, though not all, tied to communities and constituencies of color. And some of these are taking more formal institutional models such as the Nebraska Community Foundation's HomeTown Competitiveness collaborative and the work of the Black Belt Foundation in Alabama to "Take What We Have To Make What We Need." Indeed, many small rural "community foundations" as a legal model for raising philanthropic capital and increasing civic participation are not only being built upon these more informal, indigenous traditions such as giving circles and hometown associations. They are also working to support and sustain these more community-based models themselves as part of their work.

And so, the work of the National Rural Funders Collaborative has led its members to a recognition that just as the makeup of rural communities and families themselves are becoming increasingly diverse, so are its institutions—both formal and informal—that are promoting civic participation in the sense of broad civic participation and community-based giving. With this recognition comes a new understanding of the role that traditional philanthropy must play in supporting rural families and communities in their own efforts at community transformation—building wealth, increasing familiy self-sufficiency and increasing civic participation. Traditional philanthropy can no longer simply play the role of benefactor providing much-needed resources for tackling seemingly intractable local problems. Rather philanthropy must play the more supportive and collegial role of partner in helping to build and grow new local philanthropies that can be the local engines to help stimulate and sustain alternative new economies and more just social structures by which rural America's communities can not only survive, but thrive as well.

James Richardson is Executive Director and Athan Lindsay is Associate Director for Community Philanthropy and Alternative Giving, the National Rural Funders Collaborative. This multi-foundation philanthropic initiative works to expand resources for families and communities in regions of persistent poverty, especially areas where concentrations of poverty and communities of color overlap. Richardson has more than 20 years of experience in affordable housing, nonprofit management, community development lending and philanthropy, including nearly a decade with Bank of America. Lindsay formerly served as program officer for the Warner and Mary Reynolds Babcock Foundation in North Carolina. Now living in Stanley, North Dakota, Lindsay has more than 10 years experience in the field of philanthropy and was the 2006 recipient of the Association for Black Foundation Executive's Emerging Leader in Philanthropy award.

CHAPTER 4 |

Planting Philanthropy in Rural Fields

Janet Topolsky

Growing Local Giving *and* Living: Community Philanthropy in Rural Places

A new crop is emerging in rural America, quiet and steady, growing in size, scope and impact: rural community philanthropy.

Judith Johnston

The Lay of the Rural Community Philanthropy Land

In rural places across the nation, community-based philanthropy is on the rise. Exactly what distinguishes philanthropy as *community-based?* It includes any philanthropic fund created through giving and investment from local or outside sources that is dedicated to benefit a specific rural place and its people. These funds may be endowed— or not. But they must be under some form of local decision making— meaning that the fund decision makers are *based in* and *of* the community.

There are three long-standing, well-known forms of rural community philanthropy. Individual charitable giving—the donated time, treasure and talent of local people—traditionally leads this list, and is still going strong. In addition, Family and Corporate foundations dot the rural landscape, typically established by well-to-do families and firms with strong ties to the place where they started or grew their fortunes.

But newer forms of rural community philanthropy are taking hold. They offer rural people of all means the opportunity to give with meaning. The most compelling forms aim to produce specific, long-lasting community improvement. Among these new forms are:

- **Rural Donor-Advised Gift Funds.** Following the urban trend, more rural people are setting up charitable funds based at financial institutions, targeting their giving on rural places and causes.

- **Rural Hospital Conversion Foundations.** Proceeds from the sales of public hospitals to private operators have created many new "health conversion foundations" that work to improve community health, often very broadly defined, within rural service regions.

- **Rural Giving Circles.** Self-organized groups of rural givers are pooling their funds and their thinking to benefit people and organizations in their communities.

- **Rural Community Endowments and Funds.** Perhaps the greatest promise lies in the recent rapid development of rural community funds, usually held in some form by community foundations. These funds, the focus for the rest of this article, can strengthen a new and promising field of practice: Rural Development Philanthropy.

Rural Community Endowments and Funds

Rural community endowments or funds (used interchangeably in this discussion) are typically organized in one of two ways—as a free-standing independent community foundation or as a geographic affiliate of an existing "lead" community foundation headquartered elsewhere.

Why do Community Endowments matter in rural communities?

- **They create a local capture mechanism for philanthropic dollars.** Often, rural communities have no existing mechanism that allows them to "give back to the community." As a result, rural people often give—especially legacy gifts—to an alma mater the next state over, or to some national organization fighting disease. Having a community endowment can capture some of that philanthropic leakage for hometown benefit.

- **They enable rural communities to leverage other resources into the community**—for example, by providing a local fiscal agent, or a local match that attracts funds from some inside or outside source.

- **They build community assets.** Yes, financial assets are important. But as important in rural areas are the community fund's help in building organizational assets (the community endowment plus the nonprofits it helps strengthen); leadership assets, in the form of the board, advisory committees and volunteers that the community fund energizes in the community; and action assets, when it incubates or operates essential programs to address persistent problems or emerging issues.

- **They give local people the control over the strategic direction the community endowment takes,** as well as the geographic freedom to create and address a "region that makes sense." This is amazingly critical in rural regions where neighboring and overlapping jurisdictions share challenges and opportunities but have no governance system to address them together.

- **They build community.** Growing an endowment and determining how to do it requires that you friend-raise as you fund-raise and action-raise. Low-population rural areas must tap every resource possible to build a sizeable endowment, so they are motivated to work across class and race and culture boundaries to build them together.

- **They grow hope.** Once rural funds get going, and the resulting grantmaking and community investment begins to do good work, it can break rural communities out of a cycle of dependency. It flips the psychology in declining rural places that believe help must come from outside. By generating early small wins, and then bigger wins, community success breeds on itself into a repetitive upward spiral. In some places, the act of building endowment is indeed transformative.

How big is this Community Endowment phenomenon in rural places?

Who knows for sure, but it sure is growing. More than 50 percent of the 700-plus existing U.S. community foundations have been launched since 1990. The vast majority of these newer community foundations serve smaller cities, towns and rural communities.

More telling, perhaps, is the recent boom of rural community fund affiliates hosted by established community foundations. Growing Local Philanthropy, a 2004 survey of all U.S. community foundations conducted by my organization, the Aspen Institute Community Strategies Group (CSG), documented a dramatic growth trend in the incidence of locally governed geographic affiliate funds. Among the 241 responding community foundations (a healthy 36 percent survey response rate), 64 percent reported holding at least one geographic affiliate; collectively, they held 1,071 GCFs—and 75 percent of those GCFs were primarily rural.

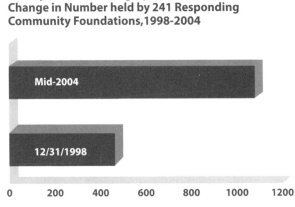

Locally Governed Geographic Affiliates: Change in Number held by 241 Responding Community Foundations,1998-2004

More to the point, the number of geographic affiliates in that sample had increased by 132 percent in under six years. Since then, plenty more have launched. In Iowa alone, state legislation helped spawn an explosion of 90 rural affiliates since the survey. CSG plans to update the survey this year.

What's causing this rural surge?

As Jeff Yost explains in the next essay, our nation is in the midst of a $41 trillion inter-generational transfer of wealth passing from parents and grandparents to…someone or something. And that transfer is taking place even more quickly in rural areas. Snaring even a small portion of this transfer into a community endowment can create a significant kitty of flexible assets for a rural place.

But other reasons contribute to this surge. Rural America is the last, best uncharted territory for urban and regional community foundations that have nowhere else to expand. Incentives from major private and family foundations (e.g., the Lilly Endowment; the Ford, W. K. Kellogg and Walton Family Charitable Support Foundations) and other donors have jump-started some rural endowments. Governments, through tax incentives and other programs, also are sparking charitable giving, sometimes even targeted at rural areas, as in Iowa.

Last, but certainly not least, rural community funds are useful, practical, flexible community development institutions that can handle all sides of a deal—whether it's convening to identify issues, organizing, leveraging or raising resources and action partners, making grants, serving as fiscal agent, even running a program if need be. Rural leaders looking for new ways to get things done have seen the light and want one in their community's tool kit!

What is different and challenging about growing
and operating rural community endowments?

Of course, most rural community endowments are relatively new and small, many struggling to maintain their footing. Five primary challenges face them.

- **Understanding endowment and philanthropic potential.** It can be harder to get community funds started in rural places, where the population typically knows little about endowments, and has limited familiarity with planned giving. Moreover, rural experience with organized philanthropy often is based on hearing about large givers in big cities. Many rural people react skeptically to the idea of building a community endowment: "Philanthropy? That's what rich people do." It takes a fund's organizers time and creativity to change this perception.

- **Growing endowment in different ways.** Some resources are held differently in rural areas than in urban. Rural families are more likely to be cash-poor and land-rich. Their average gift is smaller. To serve a small population in a large geographic area, rural funds must engage a broader base of donors to succeed—that's more staff- and time-intensive. Because the number of givers is an important metric, to grow endowment rural funds favor traditional fundraising more than metro foundations. In fact, many rural fund leaders turn the traditional endowment pyramid upside down, focusing significant effort on recruiting many small givers that will give more over the years, rather than devoting the bulk of their effort to a small set of "donors with means." Rural funds value any act of giving because it represents understanding and belief in "my community's foundation." The upside of this is what Southern Rural Development Initiative's director Alan McGregor long ago dubbed The Democratization of Philanthropy. In other words, in rural areas, everyone can be a philanthropist.

- **Developing a working business model for fund sustainability.** Seasoned community foundation leaders report that serving rural community endowments costs more than the typical fund. One reason: serving fewer people spread across a large geography adds time and travel costs to each transaction. Dealing with many small transactions magnifies this challenge. And contrary to what many think, fostering change can require extra work in rural places because wide approval of the fund's purposes and plans are critical to its success; if a few people say "no," it might not fly. So gaining initial acceptance of the community fund idea and managing the fund's initiatives in rural areas can mean a larger than average transactional effort—you have to meet with many more leaders to cross the "go ahead" threshold.

- **A working model for rural leadership sustainability.** Each rural community fund has a board, advisory groups and other volunteers involved in making local decisions. These staff and advisory boards of rural community funds are an amazing, organized, engaged AND HUGE distributed leadership network in rural America—local affiliate leaders total more than 2,000 in Nebraska alone! The challenge? They all need orientation, training, organizing, energizing—and replacing when their terms are up. Efforts to help this leadership base are ad hoc, sporadic and largely local. So much untapped, underutilized power for positive change!

- **Becoming a community change agent.** The largest challenge facing this legion of rural community fund leaders: Endowment for What? It's a lot harder to learn how to use financial assets to help communities change for the better than it is to build the assets in the first place. The emerging rural leadership network seeks help on a huge learning curve for good methods to understand the dynamics of their economies; to bridge race, culture and class in their work and make inclusion their hallmark; to make grants, run programs, convene, broker and leverage for positive community change.

What's next on the opportunity-scape?

Danger and opportunity abound here. Rural community funds could grow up to be standard-issue, primarily donor-focused U.S. community foundations unless we seize the day now.

At the first international gathering of community foundations in Berlin a few years back, Emmett Carson of the Silicon Valley Community Foundation offered a vision for emerging community foundations in other countries that is just as applicable to rural community philanthropy in the U.S. In the States, he said, community foundations are just a field—but community foundations outside the U.S. are becoming a social justice movement.

Emerging inspirations and precedents offer great hope for rural community funds over the next decade. Among them are a set of rural-focused community foundations that strive, as my Aspen Institute colleague John Molinaro maintains, not just to do good, but to do better. Among these innovative rural community change pioneers are the Nebraska Community Foundation with its nearly 100 community affiliates and companion *HomeTown Competitiveness* program; Wisconsin's Community Foundation of South Wood County, which helps lead a comprehensive *Community Progress Initiative* in a region wracked by industry exodus and decline; the Black Belt Community Foundation, which has brought community leaders together in new ways across race, class and geographic lines to "take what we have to make what we need" in the heart of Alabama; Humboldt Area Foundation, which acts as the network hub for the four-county *Redwood Coast Rural Action*; the Hopi Foundation, which offers mini-grants to low-income Hopi people starting sustainable businesses; and Minnesota's West Central Initiative, which conducts business lending, workforce development and early childhood programs. Many of these efforts are documented through other essays in this journal.

Rural Development Philanthropy: inclusive, community-led processes and practices that unite the tools of community development and philanthropy to build a better and more just future for a rural place and all its people.

These foundations and others embody what many are coming to call Rural Development Philanthropy: inclusive, community-led processes and practices that unite the tools of community development and philanthropy to build a better and more just future for a rural place and all its people.

In the RDP movement, rural community funds large and small are proving what Leslie Lilly, recent president of the Foundation for Appalachian Ohio, so aptly claims: "Small [rural] foundations help stimulate abundance in places for which scarcity is endemic but opportunity is high."

Rural community funds can help other foundations localize their work
...So how can other philanthropy help advance rural community funds?

Support the capacity of specific community endowments through:
- Operating support (annual funding and endowments)
- Challenge grants (for endowment, operations, grantmaking)
- Program support
- Pass-through grantmaking
- Special assistance (strategic planning, travel, professional development, board development)
- Partnering with or converting assets from existing family or health foundations

Support tools and data for the movement that:
- Help people believe there is philanthropic potential
- Help people understand how to grow endowment
- Help community leaders pursue community change that is appropriate to their place and people
- Help do the basic everyday work of community endowments

Support learning and innovation for the movement through:
- Peer-learning workshops, networks and mentor initiatives
- Innovations that address critical structure, program and business model issues
- Study tours and exchanges
- Web resources that make it easier to find information they need when they need it
- Stories that inspire; guides that walk them through things.

Janet Topolsky is Director of the Aspen Institute Community Strategies Group. Aspen CSG helps coordinate the Rural Development Philanthropy Learning Network.

Jeff Yost

Involve Everyone to Grow Philanthropy in Rural America

To give, you must first believe. Belief must drive the mission, the cause, the community. Therefore, to grow philanthropy in rural America, we must first believe in the future of rural America.

For several decades belief in the future of rural America and our hometowns has been in short supply. The continuing out-migration of our young people is the single greatest threat to the economic viability of many of our rural communities. Today, however, information technology is making it increasingly possible to live and work wherever we want to live and work. This new-found freedom has the potential to make rural America more economically relevant than it has been in some time. And it makes "place," and the quality-of-life in that place, paramount.

With a deep understanding of the opportunities and challenges in Nebraska's rural communities, the Nebraska Community Foundation (NCF) has built a decentralized system that embraces the most essential element of community development: asset-based community building, a system born and sustained through local assets. We describe NCF as a community development institution that uses philanthropy as a tool; we're not a charity. NCF does not itself make grants; it empowers local leaders to raise and grant their own funds, in what we call affiliated funds. One of our primary strategies is to push as much power as possible to the community level while remaining an effective fiduciary agent. NCF focuses a great deal of attention on changing the mindset and the economic prospects for rural Nebraskans.

The NCF system is designed to help local leaders involve everyone in contributing to the quality of life and economic vitality of their own community. It is an inclusive system for building community endowments where every gift, no matter how small, is celebrated. By building permanent community assets, our system reaches out to help everyone deepen or rekindle their belief in the future of their hometown.

Nebraskans have a strong ethic of giving back, especially to church and higher education. NCF encourages community leaders to build on this ethic, but to also develop goals based on community and economic development outcomes. We educate and empower leaders to be more intentional with their grantmaking, stronger advocates of their agenda, and less afraid of asking prospective donors to give. By these means, NCF is helping to develop an ethic of giving to support a spectrum of needs and opportunities that make rural communities better places to live and work.

Transfer of Wealth

Capital, under typical market conditions, flows to certainty. For the past several decades, there has been a lack of economic certainty in most of our rural communities and a consequent flight of financial capital, human capital and, most importantly, hope. But even under these dire circumstances, NCF has identified and studied a community-based asset, which, if managed effectively, could help to stem the flight of capital and reinvigorate hope.

In 2001, NCF completed analyses[1] of both the magnitude and the peak of the transfer of wealth for Nebraska and each of its 93 counties. Based on those findings, NCF estimates that $94 billion will be transferred in the next 50 years in rural Nebraska (750,000 citizens). More important still is the timing, with 86 of 93 counties experiencing their peak transfer on or before 2039; 26 very rural counties will peak on or before 2014. By comparison, the peak transfer for the U.S. as a whole will not occur until sometime after 2050, if ever, as each year the country continues to become larger and wealthier. In rural Nebraska, commonly referred to as land-rich and cash-poor, engaging the middle class in estate planning is essential in order to capitalize on the transfer of wealth opportunity, and to ensure that gifts to the community are included as intergenerational wealth transfer occurs. If only a small portion of the transfer of wealth is given back to support the communities where it was made, the resulting endowments, granted strategically, could be transformational.

We use the transfer of wealth analysis to help local leaders develop goals for endowment building in their community or county. For example, Valley County, Nebraska (population 4,647) lost nearly 10 percent of its population in the 1990s. As a result of this population loss and the resulting percentage increase in the number of older citizens, the peak transfer of wealth in Valley County is likely to occur

---

[1] Based on the groundbreaking work by J. J. Havens and P. G. Schervish, *Millionaires and the Millennium: New estimates of the forthcoming wealth transfer and the prospects for a golden age of philanthropy,* Boston College Social Welfare Research Institute, 1999.

during this decade. But even with this bleak outlook, we estimate that $597 million will be transferred during the next 50 years.

For simplicity, we encourage affiliated fund leaders to set an initial endowment development goal of five percent of the projected 10-year transfer of wealth for their community or county. Therefore in Valley County, the initial goal was set at $5.97 million ($11.94 million/year x 10 years x 5 percent). We then encourage affiliated fund leaders to include both current endowment and confirmed expectancies in their calculation. By breaking down this macroeconomic analysis into smaller, more understandable terms, community leaders, donors and their financial planners can all better conceptualize, and therefore embrace, the transfer of wealth opportunity.

Six NCF community-based affiliated funds have now met their initial goal of endowing five percent of their projected transfer of wealth. Another seven have achieved at least 50 percent of their goal. Five years ago, only one affiliated fund had met this initial goal.

NCF's process of building community capacity is not linear, but rather employs a group of reinforcing strategies and tactics to help leaders succeed in their community development efforts.

Use Catalysts to Include Everyone

NCF employs other catalysts beyond its transfer of wealth analyses to help community leaders build and make their affiliated funds more sophisticated.

A founders club is one such catalyst. These clubs can take many forms. NCF encourages its affiliates to use a model whereby a gift of at least $1,000 can be paid over a period of years by dividing it into monthly payments. An additional benefit of founders clubs is that a habit of giving is formed, which will increase the likelihood of receiving an estate gift from that donor.

Another catalyst NCF employs is estate planning and raising awareness of its value among leaders and prospective donors. This is critical because a large percentage of the transfer of wealth will occur upon the deaths of individuals. In 2002, NCF participated in a survey of 6,500 rural Nebraskans. We found that 87 percent of respondents said they gave donations annually to local charities, but only four percent said they had included their community as a beneficiary in their estate plans. With this information in hand, NCF increased substantially its education and technical assistance to donors and their financial advisors through workshops and seminars.

NCF also convenes peer-learning events as an effective way to share best practices among affiliated funds and to motivate leaders to push their efforts to the next level. Due to the growth of community-based affiliated funds and requests for assistance from others throughout the nation, NCF convened its inaugural Rural Philanthropy Conference in Nebraska City, Nebraska, in February 2007. With over 90 attendees from 13 states and nearly 20 Nebraska communities, the conference provided fund leaders an opportunity to learn about the importance of the transfer of wealth, strategies for working with boards, donors and their financial advisors and how to tie endowment building efforts to community development activities. Many of the sessions were led by NCF affiliated fund leaders themselves. The next Rural Philanthropy Conference is scheduled for September 10-12, 2008, in Nebraska City. Reviews and registration information can be found on the NCF website.

Community Endowment-Building Success Stories

Today NCF's grassroots, community-led system has 199 affiliated funds (community, organizational and donor-advised funds) located in 73 Nebraska counties. These funds are led by over 2,000 community leaders. Using our transfer of wealth analysis as a call to action, NCF and its affiliated funds have received nearly 30,000 donations in the past five years. NCF has sustained at least a 20 percent annual growth rate for each of the past five years, with endowed assets increasing by 47 percent last year. Since NCF was formed in 1993, $65 million has been reinvested by NCF and its affiliated funds.

Forty-five community-based affiliates now have combined endowments and expectancies of at least $100,000. Five years ago, there were only 16. And combined assets and expectancies for 88 community-based endowments now total $36 million, nearly four times the total recorded five years ago. Bottoms-up endowment building efforts in communities of all sizes are flourishing within the NCF system. The Nebraska towns of Pender and Thurston (combined population 1,273) offer just one example among many of successfully building a community endowment. The Pender-Thurston Community Fund is using a founders club to engage everyone. Thirty-nine of 41 public school teachers have committed to giving $100 annually in perpetuity. This has led to a total of 232 commitments from current and former residents to give $100 per year.

HomeTown Competitiveness

To fulfill our mission of building community capacity, NCF co-founded the HomeTown Competitiveness collaborative, which uses the transfer of wealth opportunity as an asset-based community development strategy to create new economic opportunity to stem the tide of out-migration. HTC is a holistic, community-driven economic development strategy based on homegrown capacities, including entrepreneurship, leadership development, youth engagement and building charitable assets and endowments. HTC is a "come-back/give-back" strategy intended to rekindle residents' belief in the future of their hometown, thereby transforming community conversations, attitudes and ultimately, our willingness to give.

Through our HTC work in communities across Nebraska, we are confronting an ironic pattern of generational belief systems. Many rural adults assume the best thing they can do for young people is to encourage them to leave home for college and pursue career opportunities in an urban center. The irony is that, when asked, significant numbers of young people say that they would love to return home to raise their children near their parents. Of the more than 700 students surveyed in 2007, about 50 percent said they could see themselves living in their hometown in the future. This is especially true in communities with HTC efforts underway.

In Ord and Valley County (population 4,647), the pilot site for HTC, personal income increased 21 percent from 2000 to 2004, compared to a statewide average of 11 percent. Endowments and expectancies now total over $7 million. And most importantly, population has increased by 3 percent since 2000, the first increase since the 1930s. Many other communities, in Nebraska and in other states, are experiencing similar results by implementing the HTC framework. Outcomes range from local business coaches helping to start and expand local businesses, to more citizens running for elected office, to efforts to recruit alumni home, to increased regional collaboration.

In all of these HTC sites, endowments are being built to catalyze and sustain community economic development efforts. Most importantly, HTC is proving to be a better case statement for prospective donors because it rekindles or renews hope for the future prosperity in their hometown.

Conclusion

The Nebraska Community Foundation is achieving mission fulfillment by believing in the future of rural America. By providing local leaders with education, assistance and tools to form and implement their own agendas, we are building a grassroots system of giving and engagement. With more compelling reasons to give, new habits of giving are being nurtured among thousands of Nebraskans in dozens of communities. People are rediscovering their sense of place and reinvesting in its quality of life.

> By providing local leaders with education, assistance and tools to form and implement their own agendas, we are building a grassroots system of giving and engagement. With more compelling reasons to give, new habits of giving are being nurtured among thousands of Nebraskans in dozens of communities.

The phenomenal opportunity of capturing a portion of the transfer of wealth is entirely relevant to the rural economy. And it will have a major impact on where our children choose to live and work in the future. As a result, NCF does not adhere to a traditional community foundation business plan. A traditional model of charging an annual fee on endowed assets would take NCF many decades to build enough assets under management to underwrite even a small portion of our community empowerment work. Given the peak transfer of wealth that is looming in many rural places, this work must occur now, not in 20 or 30 years.

Jeff Yost is President and CEO of the Nebraska Community Foundation. To learn more about NCF or HTC, see www.nebcommfound.org.

Kate Wolford

Time-Tested Models in Regional Community Philanthropy

With relatively few exceptions, philanthropic resources and direct service efforts have historically focused on the population magnets of larger cities and towns. Most foundations are based in large metropolitan areas—and many towns that lie between those metro areas also lie between our country's philanthropic cracks. Given the interconnections among urban and rural economies and issues, however, foundations are wise to consider appropriate and cost-effective ways to engage in areas beyond our immediate horizon.

I am pleased that the Council is calling for an increased philanthropic presence in rural America while also advocating that the public sector do its part to make policies and investments in support of small towns and rural communities. At the McKnight Foundation, we have experience with one such model of engagement that has worked well in Minnesota. Our experience could help others find both inspiration and practical steps to build local capacity and assets in areas other than large metropolitan centers. The McKnight-supported Minnesota Initiative Foundations present a viable, time-tested model that has provided McKnight with a great return on investment and a legacy we are proud to share.

Rural Coalitions Help Minimize Effects of Rural Collapse

Although McKnight had previously funded limited charitable programs statewide, an important evolution in our rural funding occurred 22 years ago. By the mid-1980s, economic markets in farming, mining and lumber were imploding throughout rural Minnesota. Facing unprecedented challenges statewide, McKnight's directors looked for a smart way to lend a hand. Upon visiting at length with leaders and citizens in small towns and regional centers, the board determined that the people of rural Minnesota themselves possessed the knowledge and resilience to best address their own economic and community challenges—they simply needed appropriate resources, organizational capacity and a workable system to help facilitate their efforts.

In 1984, McKnight president Russell V. Ewald spoke at a rural meeting of the state's philanthropic leaders. He explained, "The McKnight Foundation is ready to commit staff time and dollars in a process which will forge a coalition of providers and funders; governmental units consisting of representatives of the state, county and city levels; nonprofit and for-profit organizations; voluntary organizations; and citizens throughout the rural areas of the state. These coalitions would be on a regional basis, as yet undefined, and would work on solutions to the many problems that abound in our rural areas. This concept is in the idea stage and we would urge your participation in its development along with your positive response to the concept and its potential."

McKnight's board and staff were confident that such a rural *coalition* could do more to help Greater Minnesota than one institution could do *alone*. They met with dozens of Minnesota's rural leaders to consider funding structures and strategies, with an end-goal both to help minimize effects of the rural economic collapse and to better prepare for the future. The result was the 1986 founding of six regional foundations, together known as the Minnesota Initiative Foundations, or "MIFs." The MIFs were established with an initial commitment of $15 million from McKnight, joined with a $2 million investment from the State of Minnesota.

As conceived, each of the six MIFs is independent, with its own specific geographic scope, board of directors and distinct identity. The initial decision to establish six separate regional foundations—rather than one statewide foundation with a rural focus—proved to be a key element of the MIFs' long-term success. A self-determined regional focus allowed each MIF to dig in deeply into its particular context, prioritizing issues and programming accordingly.

Given the speed and severity of Minnesota's rural collapse in the '80s, it was clear that grantmaking alone couldn't turn the tide. Any full-scale solution would need to save jobs, convert entire rural economies and help new business grow and flourish. So McKnight launched the MIFs as a unique hybrid, with a dual mandate split between loans to support business and economic development, and grants and direct service to support social development—each exact balance of the two designed and implemented in response to the particular needs and issues of each MIF's region.

This was somewhat risky business, admittedly, entrusting decision making and control to newly created organizations, with untested approaches to foster both economic and social development. But the approach keyed off the Foundation's *willingness*—to release constraints on resources, to make a long-term commitment and to weather the inevitable bumps in the road that come with a new organization or new approach.

With self-determination on its side, each MIF customized a business development and loan program for its own region. Across the board, the six MIFs support smart entrepreneurs through business development loans and other means, fostering a healthy regional economy grown directly from regional resources. They strengthen their local communities through work in human services, employment support, leadership development and community capacity-building. Over time, several of the MIFs have chosen to incorporate elements characteristic of community foundations, such as donor-advised funds and community funds, to further increase opportunities for harnessing local philanthropy in their regions.

Though a gamble 20 years ago, the MIFs have evolved into strong and vibrant innovators and thought leaders in their respective regions. With a 20-plus year track record of measurable results, the MIFs have also established credibility as trusted local conveners, bringing together the private sector, public officials and community leaders to forge solutions to pressing issues while creating broad opportunities in their communities.

Although I wasn't around when McKnight's directors first established the MIFs, I am delighted daily to witness impacts of the relationships we have cultivated together since then. To achieve our goals, McKnight has settled into a five-year funding cycle with each of the six MIFs, with our commitments to be put toward operating expenses, programs and endowment. This stability in periodic core funding has enabled each MIF to spend time and energy strategically while remaining flexible enough to address emerging issues as needed.

Over time, McKnight's steady commitment has also provided space and confidence for relationships among us to evolve on all sides. We have been permitted to accompany the MIFs in their work, as a sounding board, as an advisor and as an invested funder. We have had opportunities to nudge as well as reward. The partnerships' longevity and effectiveness confirm the wisdom of investing in local leadership to shape local economies and communities.

During their first two decades, the MIFs received around $200 million from the McKnight Foundation. McKnight generally offers part of its funding to the MIFs as a "challenge grant," requiring each to raise additional funds before it can receive a certain portion of McKnight's grant payment.

In line with our desire to encourage local philanthropy statewide, these matching grant challenges have also helped encourage the MIFs toward more successful fundraising. From their local regions, the MIFs have raised significant funds to support programs as well as their endowments. Combined, the MIFs have converted those contributions into some 3,000 business loans statewide totaling over $130 million; 12,000-plus grants in local communities totaling nearly $100 million; 26,000 jobs across their six individual regions; *plus* stable endowments that currently total more than $150 million, with revolving loan assets of more than $60 million.

Minnesotans in all corners of the state benefit from capacity-building direct support services and leadership training, as well as programs to provide advocacy, resources and education in support of families and communities. Throughout the state, MIF-supported business development programs create jobs and opportunities for long-term impact and diversified economic stability. Nonprofit providers are bolstered through supportive, regionwide grants and capacity-building services. And lenders are taking advantage of investing in regional economic opportunities, with emerging fields such as renewable energy quickly entering the mix.

McKnight's staff and board are committed to our mission, and care deeply about the Foundation's impact on improving the lives of others. The MIFs' efforts in Greater Minnesota are critical to our own efforts to fulfill that mission; they go places and touch people that we couldn't even approach without their relationships and leadership. Collectively, they have played a central role forging formidable local coalitions in pursuit of statewide school readiness for all children. In their home regions, they provide loan support for entrepreneurs and entire industries, helping to transform Greater Minnesota's ingenuity and rich resources into locally produced goods and services to be shared with the state, the nation and the world.

> The MIFs' efforts in Greater Minnesota are critical to our own efforts to fulfill our mission; they go places and touch people that we couldn't even approach without their relationships and leadership.

The MIFs have had a profound impact in rural Minnesota. Throughout the U.S. today, the need for similar strategic regional planning and workforce development has never been more critical. With a longtime state-based focus, McKnight invested in direct grants to rural nonprofits for years before founding the Minnesota Initiative Foundations. But by committing to this multifaceted partnership for more than two decades so far, we have maximized returns on the investments of both McKnight and the State of Minnesota, as well as the many local communities that now support—and are, in turn, supported by—the MIFs.

Maximizing Dollars to Build Local Assets

Even from their big city bases, foundations can support rural needs in many ways. As far as I know, however, the Initiative Foundations are a unique model nationally: tied over time to a committed urban foundation partner; designed to be fully independent and increasingly self-sustaining; tapping the ideas and resources of people across rural communities to address their own local social and economic development goals.

As Russ Ewald suggested in his 1984 comments to the state's philanthropic leaders, McKnight hoped such a strategy would help encourage a more robust philanthropic and social support network across Greater Minnesota. In addition to the jobs created, loans approved, grants paid and services provided, the MIFs' combined current assets still roughly equal McKnight's long-term investment—a terrific example of how one foundation can maximize dollars to build local assets.

Guided by the expertise and foresight of excellent staffs and boards of directors, the Minnesota Initiative Foundations have increased their impact year after year, addressing emergent issues and seizing opportunities. At McKnight, we believe that investing in their establishment, development and ongoing strategic efforts has made a pivotal difference in the lives of Minnesotans statewide. For any foundation considering strategies to ensure vibrant rural communities in their own regions, we hope this proven model provides a starting point and insights into the wisdom of this type of investment.

The Minnesota Initiative Foundations

- Northwest Minnesota Foundation, Bemidji
- Northland Foundation, Duluth
- West Central Initiative, Fergus Falls
- Initiative Foundation, Little Falls
- Southwest Initiative Foundation, Hutchinson
- Southern Minnesota Initiative Foundation, Owatonna

Kate Wolford became president of the McKnight Foundation in December 2006, building upon a career of establishing locally based community efforts that empower individuals to help themselves. Through grantmaking, coalition-building and policy reform, the Minnesota-based McKnight Foundation supports children and families, the environment, community vitality, the arts, scientific research and select efforts in Southeast Asia and Africa.

CHAPTER 5 |

Rural Families and Community Concerns

Growing up Rural Doesn't Have to Mean Growing up Poor: Strategies to Earn, Keep and Grow Assets

Rural people work hard but far too many struggle to meet their families' needs. Even those who can make ends meet are at risk for financial disaster. For families who lack savings or other assets that function as financial shock absorbers, a blown tire or emergency room visit becomes not just a bump in the road but a financial calamity.

The romantic vision of rural childhood is rosy-cheeks, carefree outdoor adventures and wholesome food. But for many children, growing up rural means growing up poor: Half of all rural families that have young kids are poor and one-third of rural families headed by a single parent are poor. The picture is not improving. Between 2000 and 2005, rural child poverty increased in 41 states.

Greater economic security would be within the reach of many more rural families if the successful strategies being applied in numerous locations were more widely available. These efforts help families earn enough to support themselves, keep enough of their earnings to be financially healthy, and grow those earnings to become financially secure. Across rural America, foundations, nonprofits and policymakers are investing in effective programs that help families achieve economic success.

Strengthening families strengthens communities. When families have more earnings and income, their spending boosts local businesses. When they build savings and assets, they become the homeowners and business owners who build local economies. As financial stakeholders, they are taxpayers and civic leaders, spurring better public services, education, health care, housing, Main Street businesses and jobs.

> Greater economic security would be within the reach of many more rural families if the successful strategies being applied in numerous locations were more widely available.

At a fundamental level, these linkages between the economic well-being of families and their communities are universal. However, the opportunities, challenges and solutions vary substantially. Data from the United States Department of Agriculture's Economic Research Service demonstrate that the more rural the community is, the higher the poverty rate. And, as in urban America, there is a strong link between race, place and poverty. In the Great Plains, persistent poverty is concentrated among Native Americans; in the South and Southeast, among African Americans; in the Southwest and border counties, among Hispanics.

Increasing families' financial assets is critically important in improving long-term economic prospects. Having income helps families get by. Having assets helps them get ahead. As great as the income deficit is for many families, they face an even greater wealth gap. Assets—savings, equity in a home or business, higher education, retirement accounts—mean the difference between living paycheck to paycheck and building financial stability. Having assets that can be leveraged gives families the resilience to ride out financial reversals and to invest in their own futures.

At the Annie E. Casey Foundation, we outline three strategies needed to build Rural Family Economic Success—Earn It, Keep It, Grow It. Many excellent examples of effective solutions are being implemented across the country, supported by foundations, the public and private sectors and led by capable social entrepreneurs.

Earn It

Most rural families struggle to earn enough to meet their needs because available jobs don't pay enough. Forty-two percent of rural jobs are low-skill and vulnerable to dislocation. One of every four rural jobs would not lift a family of four out of poverty even if the job was full-time and year-round. Given this, it is not surprising that a survey of 6,500 randomly selected rural residents conducted by the Carsey Institute, a research institution at the University of New Hampshire, found that 84 percent consider lack of job opportunities to be a serious problem and 73 percent would advise teenagers to move away to find better opportunities. Out-migration contributes heavily to many rural communities' struggle to remain viable.

Effective approaches to increasing families' earnings focus on helping people to qualify for a job, land and keep a job, and advance in a career. The Lumina Foundation is addressing low-educational attainment. With funding from foundations, two nonprofits, West Central Initiative, in rural Minnesota, and Southern Good Faith Fund, in rural Arkansas, are building career-ladders in high-demand sectors. The National Fund for Workforce Solutions, a joint project of the Hitachi, Ford and Casey Foundations, the United Way of America, the Council on Foundations and Jobs for the Future, will announce a rural strategy this winter.

Many funders are using program-related investments (PRIs) to increase and improve jobs in rural communities. A PRI is a social investment—a low-interest or forgivable loan or equity investment—made by a foundation to an organization aligned with the foundation's goals. The F.B. Heron Foundation is investing a quarter of its assets in such endeavors, including many rural projects. The Northwest Area Foundation created Invest Northwest, an equity fund, to help keep and grow businesses in its eight-state region.

As a consequence of low-wage employment, hard-working rural families face a 'structural deficit'—the gap between what they can earn and what it costs to maintain even the most basic standard of living. How do families close this gap? Many go without necessities such as health care or insurance. Half of bankruptcies are due to illness or medical bills. People double up to meet housing or transportation needs. Twenty-five percent of those surveyed by the Carsey Institute confirmed they hold multiple permanent jobs and 50 percent do odd jobs to make ends meet. Ten percent of rural residents receive Food Stamps (compared to 7 percent of urban residents) and 32 percent of rural children rely on SCHIP or Medicaid (compared to 26 percent of urban children).

One of the most powerful "gap closers" for rural families is the Earned Income Tax Credit (EITC), a refundable federal credit (23 states have a state add-on) that rewards work and boosts income. Targeted to families earning low-to-moderate wages, the EITC lowers or eliminates taxes owed. If a worker does not owe taxes, or if the credit is larger than taxes owed, the worker receives a cash payment (or refund) after filing a federal return.

When eligible families take advantage of the EITC, this acts as an economic stimulus for the community. In one analysis in Iowa, EITC refunds generated as much economic stimulus as the hospitality industry. While 18 percent of rural families claim the EITC—getting an average refund of $1,700—25 percent or more of eligible workers do not. Moreover, many who claim the credit pay high fees to have their taxes prepared and for "refund anticipation loans," thereby reducing the impact.

Many foundations, community groups, state and local governments are working aggressively to ensure that all eligible workers know about and claim the credit, that they do so for free or low cost, and that they are aware of opportunities to use the refund to improve their economic security. At the national level, the EITC Funders Network, including over 80 national, regional, local and family foundations, recently sponsored the first convening of current and prospective rural EITC funders.

Keep It

While it's important to get rural families on the road to higher earnings, it's equally important to acknowledge the other side of the equation—expenses. True, the cost of living is 16 percent less in rural communities than in urban communities. But rural families earn 25 percent less than their urban counterparts.

There is a high cost to being rural and poor. One problem is that rural residents often can't find affordable financial services. Many mainstream institutions have pulled out of low-income areas, and high-cost predatory lenders are filling the void. Rural residents are increasingly the target of exploitive services—payday lending, check cashing, car title loans, rent-to-own, refund anticipation loans—that result in excessively high rates for mortgages, loans and cash. Seventy percent of payday loan customers in Kentucky are lower-income residents, reflecting a nationwide pattern.

Families living on the margin often have lower credit scores, which also contributes to the high cost of being poor. Kentucky Youth Advocates found that low-income residents, compared to their higher-income neighbors, typically pay $500 more for the same car, two percentage points more to finance it, and $384 more per year to insure it. This pattern is especially evident in the rural counties of eastern Kentucky.

Good financial education and advice can help families avoid these "money traps," and the availability of affordable alternatives is equally important. For example, the Pennsylvania Credit Union Association is making affordable short-term loans available to customers as an alternative to exploitive payday loans. Finding ways to decrease the costs of basic goods and services also is vital. Bonnie CLAC (Car Loans and Credit) helps low-income families in northern New England purchase base-model new cars at favorable terms, and many other programs help families acquire affordable, reliable used cars.

Grow It

Over the long haul, having assets is what enables families to be financially successful. Asset development is the focus of considerable work in rural America, and many foundations are supporting effective programs and promising innovations. Increasingly, the road to wealth is understood as a pathway along which families progress at various rates, sometimes slipping back a step or two and sometimes catapulting forward.

Savings provide a critical cushion, but many rural families struggle to save. One quarter of U.S. households don't own enough to support themselves at the poverty line for three months. One-quarter of female-headed households and one-third of minority-headed households have zero or negative net worth.

With this in mind, communities, foundations and policymakers are developing strategies that help low-income families save for retirement, buy a house or start a small business. Individual Development Accounts (IDAs) are matched-savings accounts in which families save towards a specific asset and their deposits are matched through resources provided by government, philanthropy or the private sector. These accounts are helping many working poor families buy their first home, make home improvements, pay for post-secondary education or job training, start their own businesses and, in some programs, purchase cars or tools. National, regional and local foundations, United Ways, and the federal, state and local governments provide critical support to help operate and fund IDA programs.

The widespread use of IDAs demonstrates that low-income families can and do save, when conditions are favorable. While a terrific innovation, IDAs are not as rural-friendly as possible. The federal program, for example, doesn't allow IDAs to be used to purchase cars—a vital asset rural families need to reach jobs in areas without public transportation.

Equity in a home is one of the best paths to upward mobility, but it is complicated in rural America. While 82 percent of rural families own their homes, those homes are worth half as much as urban homes. And rural homeowners have 40 percent less equity than urban homeowners. Moreover, owning a home won't help a family prosper unless the home increases in value over time. In rural communities, this is far from guaranteed. In high-amenity areas, where housing prices are escalating, families may be priced out of the housing market. In high-poverty areas, where economies are stagnant or declining, homes may be depreciating assets.

Manufactured housing (including mobile homes) represents 12 percent of rural homes and is the fastest-growing affordable housing. But homes on leased land in a trailer park typically are not treated as real estate, are financed at a higher rate, and do not receive the mortgage interest tax benefit. Moreover, owners are vulnerable to displacement when the park owner decides to sell. One promising effort to expand home-ownership opportunities for low-income families involves helping residents of manufactured housing parks buy and manage their communities as Resident Owned Communities. This enables homeowners to improve their living conditions and stabilize their costs, and also to build equity that produces long-term stability. An initiative to make manufactured housing a better option for rural families, known as "I'm Home," is managed by the nonprofit CFED and supported by the Ford Foundation.

Small-business ownership is another important pathway to upward mobility in rural America. Seventeen percent of household wealth is business equity, second only to home equity. Philanthropy and the public sector are helping to grow entrepreneurs in several ways, improving the prospects for rural employment and economic vitality.

Many community foundations, including the McKnight Foundation-initiated Minnesota Initiative Foundations—as detailed in Kate Wolford's essay in this journal—are working to create a supportive business infrastructure in rural areas. The National Rural Funders Collaborative is investing in high-poverty communities to expand business opportunities for minority residents. The RUPRI Center for Rural Entrepreneurship is a resource on effective rural practices.

Asset building has great potential to have a lasting, long-term impact on rural low-income families' economic well-being. When low-income families have assets, they no longer struggle to ride the tide. They raise the tide, by becoming economic investors in their own futures and in their communities.

Miriam Shark manages the Annie E. Casey Foundation's efforts to apply its philosophy that "children do well when their families do well, and families do better when they live in supportive communities" to rural America. She is a Senior Associate in the Office of the Senior Vice President.

Rural Health's Unique Challenges
Call Out for Greater Foundation Support

"What's the point of having a community health center in my county if we can't get to it?"

At a regional convening several years ago, a young mother from a remote rural town in Shasta County, California, made plain that just having health care services available in rural regions is simply not enough. A lack of dependable public transportation, extreme weather conditions and considerable travel time between towns and cities, along with the growing shortages of primary and specialty care providers, are compounding factors that have created a serious health care crisis in rural America. And it's not just in health care—acquiring other human necessities that contribute to healthy bodies and minds such as fresh and affordable food products, entertainment activities, restaurants and shopping and broadband Internet access pose major challenges for many rural parts of the country.

There are unique challenges in rural health that call out for greater foundation attention and support. Rural residents are less likely to have health insurance than their urban counterparts, according to statistics from North Carolina Rural Health Research and Policy Analysis Center. Among the 41 million uninsured in the United States, nearly one in five live in rural areas. However, in states like Montana and Maine, over 70 percent of the uninsured are from rural areas. Further, rural residents remain uninsured for longer periods of time, and their chances of being uninsured for an entire year are a third greater compared to those in urban counties (20 percent versus 14 percent).

Today, one of the greatest health challenges facing Americans is our obesity epidemic, particularly among children—by 2010, almost half of all American children will be overweight, according to predictions. Yet a number of recent studies, including two by the PennState Population Research Institute, have found that the rate of childhood obesity is even higher in rural areas and growing at an alarmingly faster rate there than in urban communities. This can be directly attributed to high-poverty rates coupled with higher caloric meals, a more sedentary lifestyle and scarcity of recreational opportunities, limited or nonexistent physical education in schools, and narrower choices for consumers at grocery outlets.

Further complicating the issue of health and health care delivery today has been the recent dramatic shifts in the demographics of rural communities. The rapid growth and spread of new immigrants, particularly from Mexico and Central America, in the past 10 years has dramatically changed the landscape of rural communities across the entire country. Today, Latinos account for over 46 percent of non-metro population growth between 2000 and 2005. With a younger population and higher fertility, Latinos are now the fastest growing racial/ethnic group in rural America. In California, over half of the births statewide today are to Latino moms. And almost half of all rural Latinos live outside of the traditional settlement states of California and the Southwest.

In many places, new Latino settlement patterns are contributing to the revitalization of small towns; in others, the influx of residents is straining social norms, housing supplies and other community resources. In addition, the younger age, lower education and large family size of Latino households suggest increased demands for health and human services, including prenatal care, child care and health education/treatment programs that are culturally and linguistically appropriate.

In addition, with the rising out-migration of rural youth leaving for better prospects in urban or suburban areas, and the lower cost of living and more attractive lifestyle and recreational opportunities for new retirees, much of rural America (with the exception of Latino communities) is becoming increasingly older. This requires special attention in the planning and delivery of health and health care resources to address the special needs of an aging population, and that can enable older adults to remain independent in their own homes and prevent premature institutionalization and repetitive hospitalizations.

Overriding all of these factors and their impact on health and well-being is the growing poverty in rural regions of the country among all age groups, but especially among non-whites. According to a study by America's Second Harvest, child poverty rates are higher in rural areas than in metro areas, with a number of rural counties in the United States having three out of five children living in poverty. Fifty-three percent of African-American children under the age of five in rural areas were found to be poor. Among the rural elderly, African Americans were reported to have the highest poverty rates of any other elderly racial/ethnic group, with almost one of every two reported to be poor.

The California Endowment's Approach to Rural Health

In 1996, The California Endowment, a private, independent health foundation, was created as a result of Blue Cross of California's conversion of its HMO to WellPoint Health Networks, a for-profit corporation. Today, with assets exceeding $4 billion, the Foundation continually strives to find the most effective means to serve its mission of *expanding access to affordable, quality health care for underserved individuals and communities, and to promoting fundamental improvements in the health status of all Californians.*

However, the sheer size of the state, and its demographic and geographical complexity with its large cities and vast rural regions, make this a daunting challenge. Just as many have pointed out that "one size doesn't fit all" for rural America, this also is clearly the case for California. How can we best understand and respond to all of the health and health care issues of the country's second largest rural state in terms of population? These areas include the Central San Joaquin Valley agricultural region, which is as large and as poor as Appalachia; a far northern region the size of Washington State, characterized by remote, mountainous and high plains towns; and the vast desert regions of southern California.

Last year, Robert K. Ross, M.D., President and CEO of The California Endowment, issued a short booklet, titled *Ten Years Later…Our Impact, Learning and Saluting Our Grantees.* The following are highlights that best reflect our approach to promoting health and wellness in rural regions of the state.

A healthy community is essential for creating healthy minds and bodies.

One of the important shifts in our thinking regarding strategies for improving the health and wellness of individuals has been to expand the focus for change to include the social, cultural, natural and built environment of the *places* where they live, work, learn and play. Too often, rural regions are treated like the "third world" of America, where valuable natural and human resources are exploited for urban consumption, and returned in the form of polluted water and sewage, garbage, contaminated air, proliferation of prisons, or nuclear or other forms of waste. But rural communities can be just as guilty of creating their own environmental health hazards through deforestation, strip mining, mega-dairies and cattle ranches, and the promotion of cheap, often dangerous manual labor in agriculture, mining, meatpacking and other food-processing activities. Other factors particularly affecting the mental health of rural residents include cultural isolation and physical isolation due to geography and weather, and lack of opportunity and resources to enrich one's life.

Act locally and globally.

To achieve the desired changes in the health of a community, a dual-pronged "grassroots-to-treetops" approach is needed. Funding for resident civic engagement and local grassroots coalition-building is essential to ensure that change strategies are developed that are responsive to those most affected and that residents are motivated and informed to mobilize in a meaningful manner. Foundations should provide capacity-building and general support to strengthen statewide and national rural health advocacy "champions". Together, these individuals, organizations and coalitions combine to achieve the necessary changes in corporate behavior and public policies at local, state, and national levels that can promote healthier, more livable communities. Our Community Action to Fight Asthma Initiative is a successful example of this approach. Under this effort, funds were provided to 12 regional asthma coalitions to lead the way on environmental advocacy to reduce indoor and outdoor hazards for school-age children with asthma in the state. These community coalitions have achieved such victories as: regulating diesel truck idling, plant allergy-free trees at rural schools, establish wood-burning ordinances, and convince hundreds of Central Valley rural schools to keep at-risk children indoors by raising flags to indicate poor air quality days.

> Foundations should provide capacity-building and general support to strengthen statewide and national rural health advocacy "champions".

Think regionally.

Geo-political descriptors such as a "neighborhood" or a county are usually not the best means for assessing health conditions or determining resource needs for rural areas. A regional approach, where commonalities can be found among more natural geo-political sub-regions (sub-county, multi-county and, in some cases, even multi-state) can provide a more useful and meaningful way to understand and respond to rural conditions. The Southern Rural Access Program, a Program Office created by the Robert Wood Johnson Foundation to address the health systems of eight rural southern states over a seven-year period, is an excellent example of this approach. One clear potential benefit in this thinking is that it opens the possibility for cities, suburban, rural and rural remote communities to see themselves linked as part of the ecology of a single region, and thus can plan and organize health and health care resources and strategies more effectively and efficiently.

Seek and promote funding collaborations/partnerships.

A health-promoting community not only has access to high-quality medical care and human services, it must also have quality educational opportunity, a non-toxic natural and built environment, economic opportunity, decent and affordable housing, and a vibrant cultural and civic life for all if its residents. This provides ample opportunity for public and private philanthropy to find their niche and contribute in a collaborative way to the overall health conditions in rural communities—regardless of their particular area of interest. In our experience, community foundations are an under-utilized, valuable resource that can be the locus of collaboration with national and regional foundations for community health promotion strategies in rural communities.

Promote the use of technology.

Tele-medicine and tele-health have become critically important tools for addressing the shortage of primary and specialty care services in rural regions. While a number of challenges exist including access to broadband connectivity, insurance reimbursement, and efficiently using time and personnel, there is no question that this technology is key to helping resolve the health care access inequities that exist for rural residents. New technologies in home health care, translation services, interactive e-health information and support not only benefit the health consumer, they can also help to build and nurture vibrant rural communities where family doctors and rural hospitals and clinics can feel confident that they have access to the latest diagnostic tools and information. Residents, particularly as they grow older, can also be assured that they don't need to leave their home or community when in need of care or services.

The California Endowment is a health-care conversion foundation. With few exceptions, health conversion foundations are chartered to spend their money on health and health care, and usually within a designated geographic region. As of 2006, according to Grantmakers in Health, there were 185 conversion foundations nationally, with assets totaling $21.5 billion, and this number is expected to grow. Given how and why health conversion foundations have been created, I firmly believe that these foundations must be held to a higher standard of accountability for how responsive they are to addressing the pressing health and health care needs of vulnerable populations—including those in rural areas. As such, The California Endowment, along with our sister conversion foundations in the state—The California Health Care Foundation,

The California Wellness Foundation and The Sierra Health Foundation—has established itself as a valuable resource for rural communities to seek appropriate and responsive solutions to their health needs.

I urge other foundations—but especially the health conversion foundations—in the country to take the leadership in increasing their philanthropic response to address the health and health care needs in their own regions. Rural health advocates also must be vigilant that the resources of these foundations are distributed equitably to rural areas. We must keep them accountable and work to make sure they, as well as all foundations, are doing their part to help rural America. Our health depends on it.

Mario Gutierrez is the Director of Rural and Agricultural Workers Health Programs for the California Endowment, where he has been spearheading its rural health philanthropy for the past 11 years. Prior to joining The Endowment, he served as a Program Officer with the Sierra Health Foundation and was Executive Director of the California Rural Indian Health Board. He is the Grantmakers in Health 2007 recipient of the prestigious Terrance Keenan Leadership Award in Health Philanthropy.

Helping Rural America Bring
Global Warming Solutions to Market

Global warming presents the greatest challenge faced by humanity today. Emissions of heat-trapping carbon dioxide (CO_2) and other greenhouse gases (GHGs) are growing faster than previously projected. As the mounting effects become apparent in people's daily lives, climate change has appropriately and necessarily emerged as a growing priority of philanthropy.

Without GHG emissions reductions of 80 percent to 90 percent by mid-century in the industrialized world, the scientific community predicts that temperatures will likely exceed the observed temperature range over the past several hundred thousand years—and thus, scientists cannot rule out widespread economic disruption and destabilization of human societies and communities. Ironically, the consequences of global warming risk unraveling the very economic, social and environmental gains of our era that philanthropy has helped foster.

Rural communities and economies will bear significant impacts from rapid warming, some of which are already evident: decline of natural ecosystems and benefits they provide; increased frequency and severity of drought and flooding from more severe storm events; greater risk of wildfires; and growing incidence of pest and invasive species infestations, to name a few.

However, seeds of rural opportunity exist amidst the peril. While aggressive energy efficiency must be our first and greatest priority in reducing CO_2 emissions, massive investment in low-carbon energy development will be required to stave off the worst consequences of global warming. This investment can become an economic engine that helps reverse the long, slow demographic death in rural regions like the Great Plains by expanding employment, improving wages and revitalizing communities.

Our Global Predicament

Fossil fuel combustion since the onset of the Industrial Revolution and human modification of ecosystems and landscapes have pushed atmospheric concentrations of CO_2 to a level not seen for the last 650,000 years. Consequently, we are moving outside the range of human historical experience and adaptation.

Our country has a disproportionate responsibility to lead in reducing emissions and reversing this trend. U.S. per capita CO_2 emissions are double Japan's and the European Union's, five times China's and 20 times India's. Meaningful U.S. action will do much to encourage others to follow suit, especially rapidly growing developing countries.

This is an urgent matter, as the CO_2 emissions growth in developing countries almost staggers belief. Coal use in China offers a dramatic example. China currently builds the equivalent of two 500-megawatt (MW) conventional coal plants every week, installing in the last three years alone coal-fired electric generating capacity equal to roughly two-thirds of the whole U.S. coal fleet. In just one year, China adds coal plant capacity equivalent to the United Kingdom's entire electrical grid. And in less than one year, China's coal plant construction locks in enough CO_2 emissions to cancel out the climate benefits of all the world's installed wind energy generation capacity.

Clearly, we must begin immediately to transition the global economy to greater energy efficiency and declining absolute CO_2 emissions. The scale and urgency of this task has begun to erode the traditional ideological contours of U.S. energy policy debate. While perennial questions of fossil versus renewable energy, large-scale versus small-scale energy production, and corporate- versus local-ownership remain, there is growing recognition that we need all safe and reliable low-carbon energy options and that we must deploy them as quickly as possible.

Rural America's Global Warming Solutions

Rural states and regions have great potential to bring global warming solutions to market and become America's dominant supplier of low-carbon energy and provider of CO_2 management services.

First and foremost, the bulk of our nation's renewable energy resource potential resides in rural America. The theoretical potential of wind power alone far exceeds total electricity demand in the U.S. economy today. Overcoming transmission capacity and other constraints to delivering wind power from distant rural areas to metropolitan markets can make wind-generated electricity a significant portion of the overall U.S. power supply. Wind farms have already become an important "second crop" and stimulus to local rural economies where capacity remains to integrate new wind power on the grid and where states have shown leadership in establishing renewable electricity standards and related policies.

Similarly, existing and emerging technologies will allow today's biomass economy to expand beyond traditional biofuels made from corn, soybeans and oilseeds to include native perennial grasses, crop residuals like wheat straw and corn stover, hybrid poplar, and others. Used to replace petroleum in liquid fuels, electric power generation, chemicals and advanced materials, these "cellulosic" feedstocks promise a much larger, more environmentally sustainable biomass supply and lower greenhouse gas emissions in converting them to useful energy and products.

Rural states also have the majority of the nation's coal reserves. Although CO_2 emissions from conventional pulverized coal power plants pose a major threat to climate stability, proven gasification technologies lend themselves to carbon capture and geologic storage (CCS), while dramatically reducing mercury and other harmful emissions from coal. Indeed, CCS has already been deployed at commercial scale in the U.S., Canada, Europe and North Africa, with millions of tons of CO_2 annually being safely and permanently stored deep underground in oil and gas formations.

Accomplishing the transition to CCS is of utmost urgency, given rising global CO_2 emissions from coal, the dominant role coal plays in power generation worldwide, and the lack of comparably scalable renewable energy alternatives in the near- to medium-term. Rural America is poised for global leadership on this front, and the successful deployment of CCS will have the added benefit of sustaining a coal-based energy sector that provides among the very highest-paying jobs available in many rural states and communities.

Finally, due to widespread opposition to new energy development of any kind in populated areas, rural America will need to host the lion's share of our nation's future low-carbon energy infrastructure of wind farms, power plants, power lines and CO_2 pipelines. For example, Midwestern governors recently committed to meeting 30 percent of regional demand for electricity from new renewable sources by 2030. If accomplished primarily by wind power alone, meeting this target will require building roughly 80,000 standard 1.5 MW commercial wind turbines on the landscape. The bitter, years-long battle over siting just one offshore wind farm near Cape Cod underscores the difficulties in meeting low-carbon energy production goals primarily through development in urban states.

A Role for Philanthropy

How much and how rapidly we transition to a low-carbon energy system will determine the level at which we stabilize atmospheric greenhouse gases and the ultimate severity of future global warming impacts. Philanthropy can play a strategic role in helping rural America to accelerate that transformation and mitigate future consequences of climate change.

Increased philanthropic investment and development of local philanthropic capital is urgently needed in those rural states with the greatest low-carbon energy potential—many of which have among the lowest per capita foundation assets.

A number of rural states are positioned tantalizingly on the cusp of the low-carbon energy revolution, but they remain relatively untouched by institutional philanthropy and increasingly left out of the explosive growth in America's foundation asset base. Several Plains states in particular have an abundance of energy potential amidst philanthropic poverty, but my own state of North Dakota most starkly illustrates this reality. The state recently ranked 50th—dead last—in per capita foundation assets. At the same time, North Dakota is America's premier renewable energy source, ranking number one in potential for both wind energy and perennial grass biomass. Moreover, the state has pioneered the largest CO_2 storage project in the world, capturing nearly three million tons of CO_2 every year from coal.

Greater philanthropic engagement in rural states can help unlock years of stagnation on federal energy and climate policy in the U.S.

Rural states' political clout in the U.S. Senate parallels their national energy importance—but until recently, foundation investments largely ignored the reality of this influence. Several energy-rich but foundation-poor states have powerful and respected senators whose votes are essential to securing federal legislation that addresses global warming. Underscoring this influence, Montana Senator Max Baucus recently cast a decisive committee vote in favor of federal CO_2 regulation, a vote which carried extra weight given that Montana has one-third of the nation's coal reserves.

Grantmaking needs to engage mainstream constituencies and traditional industries in rural states in order to build the long-term political and technology base for deep GHG emissions reductions over time.

Since the 1970s, the philanthropic community has primarily supported energy and environmental policy and advocacy oriented to the economies and political preferences of the coasts, a strategy that has reinforced skepticism and anxiety over climate change policy in rural "red states." Fortunately, grantmakers are increasingly expanding beyond the environmental community's New England and West Coast strongholds and beyond a near-exclusive emphasis on promoting renewable energy and energy efficiency. They are undertaking authentic, locally rooted strategies that engage energy industry and agricultural constituencies in a broader-based agenda.

Results of an initiative by my organization, the Great Plains Institute, shows how a broader approach, one more tailored to regional needs and realities, can bear fruit. In 2001, with funding from the Joyce and Bush Foundations, the Institute brought together representatives of the coal and utility industry, production agriculture, environmental organizations, and state and provincial governments to launch Powering the Plains (PTP). Long at odds with one another, these PTP stakeholders began a multi-year effort to build a broad-based energy and climate consensus that resulted in a 50-year regional "energy transition" roadmap. This blueprint prioritized energy efficiency and renewable energy, to be sure. Yet it also included aggressive strategies for deploying advanced coal technologies with CCS that reflect the reality of the Upper Midwest's coal dependence and coal's importance to the regional economy.

This comprehensive and politically calibrated approach became the foundation for historic energy and climate accords signed by Midwestern governors in November 2007. These accords represent the first time that Midwest rural and industrial heartland states joined the coasts in applying pressure on Washington for action on global warming. The roots of that success lie in the patient capital of foundations willing to embrace new partners and new ways to foster climate-friendly uses of coal, together with renewable energy and energy efficiency.

Foundation philanthropy needs to expand its traditional emphasis on education, advocacy and policy development to include robust and creative strategies for technology demonstration and commercialization.

Philanthropy in the energy and environmental realm has traditionally operated on the assumption that good public policy drives technology commercialization and that sound analysis and effective advocacy will generate support for such policy change. However, the reverse is equally true: Successful and visible commercial deployment of an advanced, low-emission technology can dramatically increase support for adoption of the policy incentives and regulations required to mainstream that technology.

Clearly, the private sector and governments have the greatest role to play in technology development and commercialization. But foundation philanthropy can make a strategic difference. Larger foundations have the capacity to use direct program-related investments or grants to help bring technologies to market faster or to encourage their demonstration and deployment in specific local and regional contexts, much as new technology-oriented philanthropists in Silicon Valley and elsewhere have begun to do. Foundations both large and small can also catalyze and help underwrite the kinds of strategic partnerships between governments, the private sector and nongovernmental organizations (NGOs) that spur and accelerate innovation and overcome political, social and other barriers to commercialization that private and public investment alone might not accomplish.

In conclusion, those rural places that stand both to contribute and benefit the most from building America's low-carbon energy economy tend to be relatively untouched by institutional philanthropy, both in relative and absolute terms. The scope for impact is large, and with the right leadership, policy and technology conditions—all variables that foundation philanthropy can constructively influence—rural states and regions can play a decisive role in bringing global warming solutions to the market here in the U.S. Rural America can also influence by example the energy path that major developing countries like China and India choose to follow as they meet their populations' needs and desires for higher living standards.

Actions will speak more loudly than words in this regard. We have precious little time to waste.

Brad Crabtree is program director at the Great Plains Institute, where he staffs regional energy and climate initiatives involving governments, industry, agriculture and NGOs. Crabtree also raises cattle and sheep with his wife and daughter on their ranch in North Dakota.

Foundation support helped lead to the historic signing in November 2007 of the Midwestern Greenhouse Gas Reduction Accord. Signatories included, from left to right: Premier Gary Doer (Manitoba), Gov. Chester Culver (D-Iowa), Gov. Jennifer Granholm (D-Mich.), Gov. Tim Pawlenty (R-Minn.), Gov. Mike Rounds (R-S.D.), and Gov. Jim Doyle (D-Wis.).

Rachel Tompkins

What Philanthropy Ought to Know about Rural Education

Rural America is not disappearing—but it is changing, and doing so dramatically in some places. For example, contrary to what might be expected, rural student enrollment is growing.

That's a major conclusion from *Why Rural Matters 2007*, the fourth in a series of reports by my organization, the Rural School and Community Trust, which focuses on the status of rural education in each of the 50 states. The report gives a snapshot of the conditions faced daily in every state by rural teachers and communities. Working in these communities for over 10 years, the Rural Trust has witnessed firsthand the challenges they face and the strengths they have. Our report highlights the realities and complexities of rural education in America—and the findings always surprise people, even those, such as state and national policymakers, who ought to know.

Increasing Diversity, Poverty Impacting Rural Education

Though some rural areas still suffer from declining enrollment, overall rural school enrollment increased by close to 1.4 million students between 2003 and 2005. In 2006, almost 10 million students attended schools in U.S. communities of under 2,500, accounting for 22 percent of the total national public school enrollment. The largest growth occurred in areas close to metropolitan areas, but remote rural regions also saw growth. And the pattern is not entirely what would be expected: While the Plains states are losing enrollment by a few hundred a year, the largest losses during this two-year period are in New York, Wisconsin and Missouri.

In addition to increasing rural student enrollment, we also found that rural minority enrollment increased much faster than total enrollment. Over the past decade it increased 55 percent, and some states showed increases of over 100 percent. The most diverse student populations are concentrated in states where rural education is not likely to be a primary focus. More than half of the 2.2 million minority students attend schools in one of six states: Texas, California, North Carolina, Georgia, South Carolina and Florida.

The third major conclusion is that rural English Language Learners (ELL) more than doubled in the 15-year period between 1990 and 2005—a rate of increase more than seven times higher than the rate of increase for total student enrollment. In New Mexico and Alaska about one in three rural students qualifies for ELL services; in Arizona and California, one in five. In the 11 Southeastern states, the ELL population grew by 66 percent. While the numbers of students in the region remains small, their concentration in a few districts creates major challenges for instruction.

Rural schools with larger ELL populations also tend to have higher levels of poverty. Which brings us to the fourth major conclusion: Rural poverty continues to be an enormous deterrent to school success. The poorest rural students live in the poorest states (those with the least taxable resources.) In three states, New Mexico, Mississippi and Kentucky, more than one in five families live below the poverty line. Thirteen other states have more than 15 percent of families in poverty. Many of these states also have low levels of adult educational attainment, meaning there is likely less interest in supporting public schools and likely less ability to support them.

The report also considers outcome indicators: National Assessment of Educational Progress scores for reading and math and graduation rates. Again, states in the Southeast, central Appalachia, the Mississippi Delta and the Southwest have the worst outcomes for rural students. Graduation rates are also lowest in the Southeast, with South Carolina last in the nation. Only 55 percent of South Carolina eighth-graders graduate high school five years later.

The states where rural schools produce the worst student achievement outcomes face an uphill battle to reverse the trend. They serve student populations with the severest socio-economic challenges—especially high-poverty levels—and they operate with less money than rural schools in other states. Poverty, fiscal incapacity, low levels of adult education and low levels of student achievement run in the same mutually reinforcing circles in these states, many of which are as fiscally challenged as their citizens and schools.

States do not have much control over poverty, demographics and the size or remoteness of rural student populations. But they do have control over policies like the adequacy and equity of funding, the size of schools and districts, and salaries paid to teachers. And here the picture is not very positive.

States with the lowest expenditures for students are the same states in the Southeast that have the greatest challenges. The largest schools in the largest districts are in the Southeast. A growing body of research indicates that low-income students tend to have better learning outcomes in smaller schools. They also stay in school and graduate at higher rates than low-income students in larger schools. This is one reason why so much urban school reform is focused on smaller, more personalized learning situations.

Why Rural Matters 2007 includes a map of priority rural education regions (reprinted here on page 101) based on an average of all 23 indicators used in the report. The top quartile of states have challenging populations of rural students, few resources and poor outcomes: Alabama, Arizona, Florida, Georgia, Kentucky, Louisiana, Mississippi, New Mexico, North Carolina, Oklahoma, South Carolina, Tennessee and Texas. All states have some issues of concern, but these states deserve special attention from philanthropy.

Recommended Changes to Improve Rural Education

After many years of working with educators and community members in rural communities, the Rural Trust makes several policy recommendations. First, many more dollars, both public and private, should be invested in developing good information about rural schools and rural children.

Federal policy, like No Child Left Behind, often has unintended negative consequences for rural places. This occurs because there is no attention focused on describing or analyzing education issues in rural America. The Department of Education should have an Office of Rural Education Policy analogous to the Office of Rural Health Policy (ORHP) in the Department of Health and Human Resources. ORHP constantly analyzes proposed laws and regulations to determine their impact on rural places.

The Rural Trust has just begun a new analysis of the 800 poorest rural school districts in America. They enroll about 950,000 students: 26 percent African American, 20 percent Latino and 10 percent Native American. They are in 39 states, but concentrated in 16, and the student population is poorer than that of most American cities. For those who have focused only on cities recently, one way to think of this is as New York City scattered across the nation. Understanding the characteristics of these districts and the impact of various policies on them should help us recommend even more appropriate policies and practices.

Second, keep schools small. Research here is powerful and has greatly influenced recent philanthropic investment in education. The Bill and Melinda Gates Foundation and others have invested in small charter schools and in breaking up huge urban high schools. Almost none of these philanthropic dollars are invested in rural places where small schools already exist in some of the poorest places in the country and could use help to sustain themselves and improve. Not all of these schools take full advantage of their small size to help students and families overcome the challenges of poverty.

Third, create community learning centers that combine school with other services to families in poverty and offer economies of function. Ever larger schools have been promoted in rural places for decades in order to capture economies of scale. Bigger is better, small is too expensive and local people are not smart enough to run their schools—that is the persistent mythology. Economies of scale can be achieved by developing multipurpose facilities that combine early childhood, adult education, libraries, health clinics and many other functions in the same building as the school.

> Almost none of these philanthropic dollars are invested in rural places where small schools already exist in some of the poorest places in the country and could use help to sustain themselves and improve. Not all of these schools take full advantage of their small size to help students and families overcome the challenges of poverty.

Philanthropic dollars could help with planning and overcoming the bureaucratic barriers to such collaboration. Models exist in many communities and are featured on our website, www.ruraledu.org. These models are particularly relevant in regions of declining population and school enrollment.

Fourth, maximize rural school effectiveness and efficiency with technology. The E-rate, for example, is a fund created from fees charged to telephone users that reimburses schools in low-income areas for certain communications expenses. It has provided most rural schools with high-speed Internet connections. The continued expansion of broadband services to every nook and cranny of the U.S. will connect the rest. Emphasis today should be on matching appropriate uses of technology to instructional needs and on professional development of teachers to use the best practices.

In addition, while states and localities will continue to provide the lion's share of funding for public education, making improvements to three federal policies are essential for rural districts:

Fair Title I funding for small poor districts—Title I provides $12 billion to schools based on a complex formula that sends more dollars per student to larger districts. About 950 large districts benefit at the expense of 10,000 smaller and often poorer districts. This discrepancy can be fixed without harm to the larger districts with a change in formula and a modest increase in funds.

Regional rural teacher development consortia, including higher-education institutions, education service agencies, school districts and other resources—Rural districts need help with recruitment, mentoring, evaluation and retention of teachers. Rural teachers earn 86 cents to the dollar of urban and suburban salaries, meaning the best often leave after a few years. Multi-year demonstrations that include pay incentives, mentoring, coaching, evaluation and leadership development are needed to determine the proper mix of policy and practice to overcome the problems. Only the federal government has the resources to conduct such demonstrations.

Greatly expanded ELL funding—Most rural school districts with expanding ELL populations receive no federal funding. Many states have no categorical resources to help districts with changing demographics. While these states need to provide resources to the changing districts, this is a national problem requiring federal government attention.

Rural America is complex; the issues affecting its schools will not be solved by simple solutions. But 10 million rural school children, many of whom reside in the poorest places in America, deserve the thoughtful attention and the considerable resources of philanthropy.

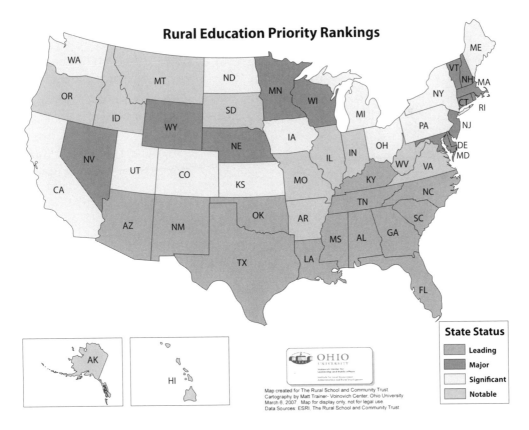

Rural Education Priority Rankings

State Status
- Leading
- Major
- Significant
- Notable

Map created for The Rural School and Community Trust
Cartography by Matt Trainer- Voinovich Center, Ohio University
March 6, 2007. Map for display only, not for legal use.
Data Sources: ESRI, The Rural School and Community Trust

Rachel Tompkins is President of the Rural School and Community Trust.

John Beineke

Martha Lamkin

Taking Chances: Helping Break Down Barriers of Rural Educational Access

In 1967, a year before his bid for the presidency, Senator Robert F. Kennedy visited the Mississippi Delta. Social services, health care and education were inadequate to meet the needs of the population. The poverty he witnessed firsthand, especially with children, changed him. He returned to Washington, D.C., a different man.

Today, the Delta in both Arkansas and Mississippi remains a challenging place to live and work. In fact, a recent lawsuit brought by a rural Delta school district demonstrated a stark disparity between funding for rural and suburban schools in Arkansas. The case, won by the Delta school district just last year, led to an infusion of resources into many disadvantaged districts and school consolidations throughout the state.

The 'RIGTT' Test for Funding Grants

Robert Sparks, physician and former president of both the W.K. Kellogg Foundation and the California Association of Medical Foundations, created what he has called the "RIGTT" test for funding grants. This acronym stands for:

- **R** – Is the idea RIGHT—appropriate and accurate in purpose, benefit and detail?

- **I** – Is the idea IMPORTANT—a high priority for society now or in the future?

- **G** – Is the idea GOOD—Will the activities benefit a clearly identified group of people and potentially alleviate an identifiable problem?

- **T** – Is the idea TIMELY—Is the community ready to embrace the idea and work toward a solution of the issue?

- **T** – Is the idea TRANSFERABLE—Can the idea be transferred to a similar group or setting and find success in its implementation?

With these markers in mind, Arkansas State University began to seek ways to break down the barriers of educational access for youth in the Delta. Leaders sought advice from educators and practitioners on what changes were needed to halt the region's downward educational and economic spiral.

Through work with the National Rural Funders Collaborative (NRFC), a handful of foundations are working to address issues of persistent poverty in rural areas. Lumina Foundation, an NRFC partner, was introduced to this work just a few years ago. With Lumina Foundation's focused mission on improving access to post secondary education, the Foundation's staff looks for areas that are open and ready for change. The Arkansas Delta fit this model: state policies were in place to support a change effort, a strong university partner wanted to implement well-tested programs, and local education leaders were calling for change.

For all of these reasons, Lumina Foundation decided to invest grant funds in the Delta region. Few foundations have risked taking on the systemic and generational challenges of this region. But Lumina Foundation ventured into one of the lowest socio-economic areas of the nation to do what foundations are supposed to do— take chances, invest in change and make a difference.

Educational Renewal: A Daunting Task in the Delta

To lead the effort, Arkansas State University (ASU), a modest-sized regional university, served as convener and catalyst for seven school districts. Located in Jonesboro, ASU is a geographic and demographic demarcation point. To the northwest of Jonesboro are the beginnings of the rocky foothills of the Ozarks—a region with little racial diversity but considerable poverty. Fifty miles to the southeast is another low-income area, but one with a significant African-American population—the rice- and cotton-growing region of the Mississippi Delta.

The task of bringing educational renewal to these regions is daunting. Arkansas ranks 49th in the nation in the percentage of its population holding a bachelor's degree. Clearly, increasing access and success in higher education is an urgent need in the state—and we know that students who earn college credits in high school and participate in a rigorous curriculum are more likely to go to college and to graduate with a degree.

The purpose of the Lumina Foundation grant was clear: to enhance college access and success for rural and minority students in the Arkansas Delta by increasing their involvement in the College Board's Advanced Placement program, which exposes students to college-level coursework—and allows them to earn college credit—while still in high school. In addition, other efforts were made to give students and parents a clearer vision of higher education.

The Lumina Foundation grant provided the seed money to create an Advanced Placement Institute at ASU. One of the major reasons that students in the Delta did not have access to AP classes was that teachers had little access to AP training. One element of AP, beyond the more rigorous courses and college credit for superior students, was the idea that AP instructional strategies would be good for all students in all classes. In a sense, "all boats would rise" if teachers had the knowledge, skills and teaching strategies to produce a more demanding curriculum for all students.

Advance Placement Institute Advances Education

After four summer Advance Placement Institutes at Arkansas State University, more than 900 teachers were trained to teach AP and pre-AP courses. Even the dean of the College of Education—who is also one author of this essay—enrolled and completed the week-long training experience in AP American History. With one year left in the grant, the successes over the past three years have been many and measurable:

- AP and pre-AP courses at the seven school sites have increased in number from 36 to 93—a 40 percent increase.

- The number of students enrolled in AP and pre-AP classes has grown from 562 to 1,455—again an almost 40 percent escalation.

- Beyond the classroom, ASU has sponsored counselor, administrator and AP coordinator workshops.

In addition to using the Advance Placement Institute, partner schools implemented other strategies. Parents and students visited the university campus, school administrators acknowledged students' academic success publicly, and faculty marketed the rigorous programs to parents and students. One of the partner schools believed that for students to capture a vision of higher education they might need to actually *experience* higher education. So a select number of students at this public high school were offered scholarships through this grant program allowing them to enroll in a community college class. The opportunity for a real-life encounter with the college environment was another motivation for the students to see they could succeed.

The first three years of the grant have been used to build the foundation for student success. Data for the final evaluation of the project are now being collected, so it is a bit too early to share specific, quantifiable lessons. Still, there are some general points worth sharing. First of all, we do know that students who were not on the academic track in the ASU project are now enrolling in AP classes and seeing that higher education is indeed possible for them. Second, it seems likely that, if this project can show progress in this rural, diverse, economically disadvantaged region, then successes can also occur in other parts of the nation. Even if those regions lack financial resources, success is achievable so long as they are rich in other resources—such as universities and the ability to set high expectations for students.

> It seems likely that, if this project can show progress in this rural, diverse, economically disadvantaged region, then successes can also occur in other parts of the nation. Even if those regions lack financial resources, success is achievable so long as they are rich in other resources . . .

Sustainability is critical for any grant. Each of the schools now offers an array of AP classes, taught by instructors who have honed their skills at the ASU Advanced Placement Institute. In addition, the state of Arkansas has bolstered the AP programs in the Delta and the state by paying for the AP examinations. Finally, the university's Advanced Placement Institute is now self-sustaining for the foreseeable future.

This project met the RIGTT test put forth by Dr. Sparks. Culture and attitudes are slow to change, but through ASU's Advance Placement Institute, more students are being exposed to college, more teachers are trained to provide rigorous curriculum, and students know that college is an option for them. It's a promising start to helping break down barriers of educational access for youth in the rural Delta.

Dr. John Beineke is Dean of the College of Education and Professor of Educational Leadership and Curriculum, Arkansas State University, and formerly a program director at the W.K. Kellogg Foundation. Martha D. Lamkin is the former President and CEO of Lumina Foundation for Education.

CHAPTER 6

Profiles of Philanthropy's Persistence, Leverage

Helping Rural Areas Reinvent
Philanthropy to Serve Their Own Needs

Since 2002, the Arthur M. Blank Family Foundation, based in Atlanta, has made grants totaling nearly $1.7 million to 55 nonprofit organizations in southwest Montana, to improve quality of life for residents of Park and Gallatin counties.

Our experience in Montana—one of the 10 states that make up the Philanthropic Divide—reveals the untapped potential for growing philanthropy in rural, underserved states. Our experience also persuades us that the best service outside foundations can provide is in helping these states adapt and reinvent philanthropy. We should not assume that underserved states can—or ought to— build philanthropy by mimicking the practices found in other places.

John Bare

When Arthur Blank bought the Mountain Sky Guest Ranch in Paradise Valley, his instincts told him that he and his foundation staff were ill-equipped to make meaningful grants in rural Montana from their offices in Atlanta. Further, he recognized several important characteristics of his young ranch hands, the individuals who wrangle horses, clean cabins and prepare gourmet meals during the guest season. They were caring; they were smart; they had roots in the nearby communities and they wanted to make a difference.

Penelope McPhee

He charged them—the wranglers, the housekeepers and the chefs— with the task of figuring out what the needs were in the community and what they could do with limited resources to have an impact. He gave them a free hand—and the support of a professional philanthropy staff in Atlanta. Together, the ranch staff and the foundation staff have been learning, experimenting and inventing a new breed of philanthropy. The participants are still charting the characteristics of Mountain Sky Guest Ranch Fund's (MSGR) relatively young giving program, but several parallel the experience of other rural philanthropists: Flexibility, collaboration and respect for local knowledge and nonprofit capacity are chief among them.

From the home office in Atlanta, our challenge has been to support the Montana process. Local demand drives everything, so the burden falls to us to have a deep understanding of what our colleagues need. Based on our understanding of the demand of the local community, we were able to provide MSGR Fund staff with access to philanthropic tools and approaches, with the express intent of adapting and reinventing them for their setting. The trick is avoiding any bright-line tests. It's wrong to assume underserved areas cannot benefit from assistance from traditional foundations. It's also wrong to assume these communities should copy what we've done in Atlanta, Phoenix or coastal South Carolina.

Rural Areas' Great, Untapped Potential and Strong Desire for Results

In seeking to build philanthropy in rural America, we are reminded of the caution that has emerged through decades of anti-poverty work: It is a mistake to assume that the people themselves are flawed in some way; that they need to be fixed or repaired. Foundations seeking to build philanthropy in rural America may find what we have discovered in working in southwest Montana: that there is great, untapped human capital on the ground.

It is likewise a mistake to assume that an underdeveloped nonprofit sector and a poor tradition of philanthropy translate into a deficiency of human talent. In our experience, one doesn't follow the other.

On the other hand, there are deficiencies associated with a weak nonprofit sector. In rural America, this often includes low levels of social capital. When the John S. and James L. Knight Foundation did its groundbreaking social indicators work in 1998 through 2001—tracking more than 100 administrative data and survey responses across 26 urban and rural communities where the foundation makes grants—it revealed that small-town and rural do not automatically translate to the high levels of social capital imagined in Frank Capra's idealized communities.

In Knight's work, levels of volunteerism for neighborhood and civic groups were low in Brown County, South Dakota—much lower than in places like Miami, Detroit, Charlotte and Boulder. It is easy enough to make the leap that folks in South Dakota are apathetic. The more likely explanation, in our experience, is an absence of strong neighborhood and civic groups organizing adults to volunteer and make a difference.

The remarkable strain of self-sufficiency that—for better or worse—is so much a part of rural life, particularly in the West, makes the social capital course extraordinarily difficult to navigate. In small and rural communities in South Dakota, North Dakota and Minnesota, according to the Knight data, adults showed less concern about community involvement than in other places. In short, the supply of participation in civic efforts is often low because opportunities are few. Opportunities are few because, in general, there has been weak demand for communitywide organizing.

When asked to choose the best method for improving the community—either volunteering their own time or getting others involved—more adults in these small, rural communities say the most effective approach is for them to put in their own time. (In some small rural communities in the South, on the other hand, where community organizing has a longer tradition, especially through churches, getting others involved is the preferred method.)

What we've learned at Mountain Sky is that conditions are suited for local leaders to coordinate and collaborate in new ways. There is a strong desire for results. The population is small enough for individuals to know one another easily. And leaders are coming at issues fresh, without a negative history of joint nonprofit projects. In these conditions, individuals respond to the invitation to collaborate in a way that is nearly impossible in the large, urban nonprofit environment. Not only is expertise valued, locals are in fact hungry for it, hungry to exchange experiences and to build relationships.

Contrast our experiences in Atlanta and Mountain Sky. Metro Atlanta is home to nearly five million residents. In this metro area, the Blank Family Foundation focuses one of its grant programs on improving youth fitness and reducing youth obesity. There is great complexity and variation within the nonprofit community. Our partners range from the Metro Atlanta YMCA, with an operating budget of about $100 million and an extraordinary reach across the region, to neighborhood associations that have never put together a budget until they apply for a small grant.

In an urban area, the need is so expansive and varied that foundations almost always have to segment the marketplace to identify a meaningful role in pursuing social change—and to have any hope at making an impact. New nonprofits are created all the time, and leadership turns over frequently. Everyone knows somebody else working on the same issue. But no one knows everyone. There is usually a long history of competition among nonprofits, whether competition for service-delivery contracts or purely by brand. And even if we were able to assemble a directory of everyone who cares about the issue, the size of the group would be too large to organize for a single conversation.

Rural Areas Require Different Approaches to Grantmaking

The previous snapshot of our work in Atlanta is recognizable to foundations working in urban areas where philanthropy is well established and where it attempts to work alongside government and business to improve quality of life. As a result, foundation leaders have adopted or invented various tools that help along the process of grantmaking in these situations. The basic components of philanthropy—needs assessments, grant applications, concept papers, RFPs, evaluation tools, theories of change, intermediaries, and so on—may seem universal. But in fact, most have been developed for use by traditional foundations working on national issues or in urban settings.

When the MSGR Fund staff decided to focus on improving youth outcomes in Park and Gallatin counties, it could easily wrap its arms around the entire universe of youth-serving organizations in the area. The MSGR Fund found the groups eager to explore options together and to consider collaborative opportunities. This is not to say the work was easy, but that the process of organizing local nonprofits around a compelling issue was different than it would have been in Atlanta. The MSGR Fund staff could put all the executive directors in a room—and did so, in an October 2005 workshop titled "Building a Web Instead of a Cocoon: Collaboration for Community Vitality," which drew 65 individuals representing 41 organizations for a two-day retreat. The overnight stay was critical to the success of the event, as it ensured sufficient time for authentic networking, as opposed to filling the time with didactic programs. The Fund succeeded in stimulating new grant proposals, based on new collaborative partnerships, specifically because it engaged local organizations in an authentic way and did not attempt to overlay a process that a national foundation had found successful in urban areas.

Tawnya Rupe, who wrangles horses and manages the Mountain Sky Ranch gift shop during the guest season, has led the Ranch Fund giving program since 2004. "The creativity was inspiring," she said, "and witnessing the energy in the room was indescribable as each group shared their ideas. One important note is that the majority of these youth groups had heard of one another but had never met. They openly admitted they were not referring the youth they served to other youth programs, although they should."

After the collaboration retreat, several youth-serving organizations started meeting monthly, on their own, to improve ongoing coordination and to pursue ideas that no one group could take on alone. From the retreat, these youth-serving organizations have worked on a referral system that tries to build on the successes of each program.

The idea is to provide some type of continuum of care, so that a young person who succeeds in one particular program is connected to new opportunities with nonprofits prepared to provide services at the appropriate level of need. Without this, Tawnya explains, "youth are exposed for a period of time and are then stranded without further opportunities."

Filling service-delivery gaps for the hardest youth cases has been one of the lasting impacts of the 2005 retreat. Participants were frustrated that in Livingston, the largest community in Park County, there was no program serving teen-agers who were involved in the courts system or were at the greatest risk of washing out of school. No single nonprofit organization could take on this population. A half-dozen organizations, including Big Brothers Big Sisters, worked out a collaborative effort that is reaching these kids now, giving them the skills and counseling they need to right their course.

Tawnya and the ranch team continue to innovate. Last year, the fund managers decided to add $50 to every grant check to pay the nonprofit's dues in the Montana Nonprofit Association. This seemingly small investment is helping to build local social capital as well as strengthening the statewide sector. For the 2008 grant cycle, the Ranch staff elected to invite proposals in two new areas of interest: efforts to plan, develop and maintain walking and hiking trails in Park and Gallatin counties; and programs that empower youth through the challenges of physical activity and outdoor adventure, including innovations that make use of the natural resources in Paradise Valley.

In the end, leaders hoping to grow philanthropy in under-served states should remember that rural communities have often reinvented innovations to fit their particular needs, as urban models failed to work universally.

Even after President Franklin Delano Roosevelt created the Rural Electrification Act (REA) in 1935, privately held utilities, which served cities and towns, did not respond to federal incentives to electrify rural areas, where nine of 10 farms were dark. In fact, most farms were not served until rural residents organized themselves, creating self-run electric cooperatives that survive today, serving 40 million

The narrowing of the Philanthropic Divide may well play out the same way as rural electrification did, if there is a concentrated effort to provide capital to and empower residents in underserved states, asking them to re-invent philanthropy to serve their needs. The rest of the country will benefit from this 21st century innovation.

Americans. It was these cooperatives that leveraged the REA's financing offerings. In turn, the innovation among the co-ops began to shape the practices of the power companies everywhere.

The narrowing of the Philanthropic Divide may well play out the same way as rural electrification did, if there is a concentrated effort to provide capital to and empower residents in underserved states, asking them to re-invent philanthropy to serve their needs. The rest of the country will benefit from this 21st century innovation.

John Bare is a Vice President and Penelope McPhee is President and Trustee of the Arthur M. Blank Family Foundation.

D i a n e K a p l a n

Fighting Tooth and Nail for Change:
Special Challenges in Rural Communities

Like rural communities elsewhere, dentists are rare in the remote areas of Alaska. Generally, the only time rural Alaskans can justify the expense and burden of flying a long distance to see the nearest dentist is in the case of an emergency—when they're suffering extreme pain. By then, more often than not, the tooth has to be extracted. The end result is that there are villages in Alaska where a majority of adults have no teeth due to very poor oral health care.

Alaska's children aren't faring much better. We have all seen children with bad teeth—they cover their mouths when they talk or smile, and they withdraw from social settings. Most sadly, they soon lose the will to succeed, their futures determined at much too young an age.

So what's a foundation to do to help? At the Rasmuson Foundation, we've learned that foundations must prepare for controversy and opposition in tackling entrenched problems such as poor oral health care in rural locations. Foundations must work to use their leverage beyond the delivery of grant dollars. However, despite everything you do to prepare, don't be surprised if the opposition is stronger than you anticipate. Solutions are never as easy as they might appear. No one person or entity is explicitly against improving the state of human conditions. Nonetheless, change is hard.

...foundations must prepare for controversy and opposition in tackling entrenched problems such as poor oral health care in rural locations. Foundations must work to use their leverage beyond the delivery of grant dollars.

When Pushing for Change
Is Critical and Well Worth a Fight

When the situation is as serious as dental care in rural Alaska, where the dental caries (decay) rate for the Alaska Natives population is 2.5 times the national average, pushing for change is critical. At the urging of several rural Native health organizations, the Rasmuson Foundation, along with the Robert Wood Johnson Foundation, the Ford Foundation, the National Rural Funders Collaborative and others, supported the creation of a new category of dental providers under the long-standing and highly successful Community Health

Aide/Practitioner program. For four decades, this program has served the medical care needs of rural Alaska, with Community Health Aides providing the backbone of the system. The rationale for the program was simple. If mid-level dental care providers were accessible to deliver more frequent dental procedures and surgeries, better oral health care for communities without local practitioners (or roads to bring them to the community) could be accomplished.

Five years since its inception, I am proud to say the Dental Health Aide Therapist program, run by the Alaska Native Tribal Health Consortium, is proving to be an initiative well worth the fight. There are now more than 10 therapists practicing in rural communities in Alaska. With an eye toward duplicating this success, an in-state training program was established. The W.K. Kellogg Foundation has just made a significant grant to the program. And, other foundations and communities around the country are interested in adapting the program for their rural areas.

The increasing interest has developed, in large part, because the Rasmuson Foundation and our partners have been passionately evangelical about the issue. If you'll pardon the pun, we've had to fight for better oral health care tooth and nail. At the outset, there was intense opposition from organized dentistry. The Alaska Dental Society, in conjunction with the American Dental Association, lobbied hard against the program in Congress, suggesting concerns about patient safety and standards of care—concerns we believe are without merit given the program's training and supervision by practicing dentists in the field. Until this year, we had to fly students interested in becoming dental health aide therapists to New Zealand for training. Despite the fact that the dental health aide therapist concept is accepted and actively practiced in 50 countries worldwide, no American dental school would take on the program.

Progress is being made, albeit not as swiftly as we would like. The University of Washington is the first American university to develop a curriculum for these students, although only for the first year of a two-year program. Fortunately, we have enough dentists within Alaska willing to directly teach students for the second year, allowing an all-American program. As a demonstration of the lingering opposition by the dental community, the first-year curriculum was developed by the University of Washington's medical school, NOT its dental school. Dental schools risk losing accreditation and prestige if they take part in this initiative.

There is little doubt here that it will be difficult to replicate this program elsewhere. After much legal legwork by the Alaska Native Tribal Health Consortium, the American Dental Association and the Alaska Dental Society finally dropped a lawsuit against the Dental Health Aide Therapist Program this past June and agreed to support the effort, though only in the State of Alaska. As a result, foundations will need to help other communities seeking dental health aide therapists prepare for significant opposition. Foundations must be willing to stand firm and provide support for advocacy and legal challenges, perhaps even taking on some of the work themselves. As Kellogg Foundation President Sterling Speirn notes about his foundation's strong support for the program, "Social change doesn't happen easily when you're trying to change a system and changing the rules of the game."

Leveraging Relationships for Greater Impact, More Philanthropic Support

Key to achieving success in tackling entrenched social problems is recognizing that a foundation official's personal connections with state and community leaders can have far-reaching impact. Leveraging these relationships, together with the foundation's ability to convene community leaders, can have significantly greater impact than the delivery of grant funds alone. Ultimately, I am not sure that it mattered how much we gave for the Dental Health Aide Therapist program. Our success is more a result of using our network of contacts in the public sector and public policy worlds. For every $1,000 we contributed for the effort, the Rasmuson Foundation leveraged about $5,000 in public funds. We've also helped nonprofits and grantees meet and connect with those in positions of power. That's not something nonprofits can necessarily do on their own, even with foundation funds. Foundations are often run by people with solid connections to community leaders who can influence what happens. Our success in Alaska can be directly attributed to the strong support of the State's Congressional delegation—Senators Ted Stevens and Lisa Murkowski and Representative Don Young, all long-time friends of the Rasmuson family.

In addition to support for specific issues, the Rasmuson Foundation also sees the overall importance of helping develop greater philanthropic support for rural areas, allowing these communities to push for change and address their own needs. Lack of philanthropic support is a real problem for rural areas. Most rural places do not have community foundations or funds. While rural people in general are good about caring for and looking out for each other, that's not the same as having a place that can help lead efforts to impact the community at large. That's where foundations can really help.

I regularly travel around the state and meet with local communities and nonprofits that have never applied for a grant from the Rasmuson Foundation. Most recently, I spent four eye-opening days traveling 800 miles along the Yukon River, stopping in a dozen villages and fish camps along the way. These visits help us learn about rural community needs, but more importantly, the visits help these communities by bringing residents together for a rare opportunity to discuss concerns in a neutral forum. Community members learn from one another and identify areas in which they can work together to improve their community. In addition, for 11 years now the Rasmuson Foundation, along with a dozen other local funders, has led an Educational Tour of Alaska for Grantmakers. We invite a group of national foundation leaders to Alaska to learn about philanthropic opportunities in the state. To date over $50 million has been awarded to Alaska organizations by past participants on the tour. It is a concept that I can't recommend highly enough. It is a highly effective way to help raise awareness among funders about issues facing rural America and opportunities for their help. It's one thing to say "rural" and think about cows and hayfields at the end of a dirt road. It's another to boat upriver to a Yup'ik Eskimo village of 300 and experience life in a place with no roads, no cars and no running water.

When it comes to pushing for change on a specific issue, a foundation must be prepared to ruffle feathers and handle unexpected challenges. The Rasmuson Foundation is currently exploring ways to help stem domestic violence throughout the state. This issue has unique challenges in Alaska, as victims often have no choice but to leave their community. Leaving home to pursue personal safety is complicated in rural communities. The nearest shelter is usually some distance away and often requires the added expense of air travel. Additionally, people in the community are often interconnected. The head of police could be a relative of the abuser, and more inclined to take the abuser's side, or the community's one public safety officer could even be the abuser. Over the past few years, the foundation has worked to improve and better equip shelters to provide safe harbor, as well as help victims and their families rebuild their lives. With many of the shelter facilities now improved, we are turning focus toward the programmatic side to help with the causal issues.

Based on our experience with domestic violence, our track record with improving oral health care, and with other issues, we know it won't be easy. But it's too hard—it's unfathomable—to think about doing nothing. So we must push to change the state of things to make life healthier, safer and a whole lot better for all Alaskans. That's what drives us to continue fighting—yes—tooth and nail.

Diane Kaplan is President of the Rasmuson Foundation in Alaska.

Judith L.Millesen, Kenneth Strmiska and Martha Ahrendt

Economic Renewal: Case Study of a Community Foundation as Catalyst for Change

The Community Foundation of South Wood County, together with its collaborative partner, the Heart of Wisconsin Business and Economic Alliance, has empowered a diverse citizenry in rural Wisconsin to promote responsible, collective and visionary citizenship that is transforming community culture and invigorating civic engagement. It is a story of devastation, renewal and growth. It's a story of hope, promise, resilience and pride. It's a story of what can happen when community foundations carry on a tradition of community leadership, responsible citizen engagement and philanthropic investment for the common good.

Judith L. Millesen

The story begins seven years ago in Central Wisconsin. For over 100 years Consolidated Papers, Inc., was the major employer, economic force and provider of civic leadership and philanthropic support in the county seat of Wisconsin Rapids, population 18,000.

But in the year 2000, Consolidated Papers was purchased by an international company. The new owners completely revamped the executive structure, moving top management from the local area and eliminating much of middle management. Also in 2000, the second major industry in the county, cranberry farming, was devastated by a depressed market. As the largest producer of cranberries in the world, growers from this area watched as cranberry prices sank from $88 per barrel to $8 per barrel.

Kenneth Strmiska

This one-two economic punch resulted in a loss of over 4,500 jobs in a community with total employment of approximately 12,000 people—a dramatic 39 percent reduction in employment. Not only had the economy in this community been devastated, personal attitudes and beliefs about the future had also suffered. Only three out of 56 high school students surveyed indicated they were planning to stay in the community—and these were the farmers, "tied to their land." By 2004, central Wisconsin's South Wood County was being described as a "dying community."

Martha Ahrendt

So the Community Foundation of South Wood County—a rural community foundation with assets of $18 million in 2004—facilitated a coordinated effort to transform community culture by promoting civic engagement and building social capital. The goal was to make the community more self-reliant: to put the area's economic future into the hands of the people living and working there. The foundation partnered with the Heart of Wisconsin Business and Economic Alliance to launch the Community Progress Initiative (CPI), providing a structure that would support broad-based inclusive community involvement, responsible citizenship, entrepreneurial opportunities and vigorous business growth—all the while continuing to nurture a spirit of individual philanthropic giving in support of the common good.

Among CPI's many successes: the creation of seven "industry clusters" that helped businesses find ways to collaborate, identify new markets and satisfy customers; the development of entrepreneur-assistance programs that were designed to encourage the expansion of existing businesses, provide technical assistance to start-up businesses and link owners to investment capital; and the establishment of seven community visioning and progress teams with corresponding endowed Progress Funds held by the Community Foundation.

The story of how this transformation began and continues to develop has important implications for community foundations committed to strengthening, stabilizing and empowering communities.

The Role of Community Foundations in Community Stability and Empowerment

Community foundations are a rapidly growing and influential part of today's nonprofit sector. Community foundations can play an important leadership role in improving the quality of life of their communities by stimulating and coordinating philanthropic giving while also being responsive to the changing needs of local constituents—broadly defined, to include not only donors and grantees but also partners in the public and private sectors, and even the disadvantaged and previously disengaged. Thus, in times of economic uncertainty, rapid technological change, dwindling resources and complex societal needs, it seems reasonable to expect community foundations to play a key role in building community stability and empowerment.

South Wood County is a historically economically vibrant manufacturing town and agricultural area. Yet, like so many rural areas across the United States, it is also part of a growing network of communities facing challenges related to globalization and the resultant need to reinvent a thriving local economy. Understanding the key elements of community culture, leadership, stability, empowerment, charitable giving as well as defining key roles for major players such as community foundations, government and local citizens will determine how communities thrive or fail in our global economy.

The Community Progress Initiative: Three Broad Outcomes

Learning more about and documenting the community empowerment process in South Wood County has generated important insights about how other community foundations might take the lead in stimulating economic growth and development across rural America.

CPI has been an innovative, inclusive, collaborative effort to involve citizens in building on existing resources to strengthen the local economy, create an entrepreneurial self-reliant culture and plan for the future. CPI has worked to achieve three broad outcomes through a number of specific programs and projects. First, CPI created a business-friendly culture that encourages the expansion of existing businesses, provides technical support to new start-up businesses and links owners to investment capital. Second, CPI is nurturing community leadership, relationships, networks and knowledge in ways that build a strong and positive local community. A number of innovative programs are providing community members with the practical skills training needed to achieve success and to "drive positive change."

Third, CPI is working to create an innovative, entrepreneurial, self-reliant culture by increasing capital and attracting funding. In addition to notable and generous local private philanthropic support as well as federal appropriation and grants from federal and state agencies, CPI has also attracted national attention from the foundation community. CPI has received nearly three-quarters of a million dollars in grants from the Ford Foundation to develop further the leadership skills of local residents.

The Community Progress Initiative Has
Engaged Residents, Putting Past into Perspective

CPI has been instrumental in shaping a new vision for the region, shifting the culture from one of dependence with highly concentrated power to one of self-reliance with dispersed power where equity and inclusion are valued. By way of town hall meetings, community picnics, a speaker's series, leadership training, study tours and an investment in strategic philanthropy, people are learning more about their neighbors, their communities and how others have become skilled at negotiating conflict to encourage "looking at the positives and letting go of the negatives."

Much of the success is directly related to how people are communicating across historically entrenched geographical, ideological, industry-related and socioeconomic boundaries. It's not that the boundaries no longer exist, but rather community members are finding ways to put the past into perspective. Through cross-cluster collaboratives, industry-specific networking, government partnerships, and true commitment to work and converse with people in new and different ways, the residents of South Wood County are "making it happen."

We heard stories of village boards and town boards close in geographical proximity that "for the first time ever in history" had come together to talk about common interests and shared needs. We heard stories about how people who tired of the negative attitudes and persistent cynicism have worked to engage the skeptics by listening to their concerns, focusing on common interests and encouraging involvement. The overall impression we reached was that, in general, people in the community are pleased about the change in attitude and attributed much of that change to CPI.

Lessons for Other Community Foundations or Community-Building Efforts

There is practical value for community foundation leadership throughout the country in South Wood County's experience. Moreover, the people we interviewed offered useful guidance for others who are committed to strengthening, stabilizing and empowering communities and may also be considering similar initiatives in their communities. The lessons include the following:

The value of communications—CPI organizers support access to information and transparency in communications. The initiative enjoys tremendous support from the local media, including dedicated space to promote events and provide information in the newspaper and on a local cable channel. Frequent and consistent support from the media has been essential in promoting local outreach and keeping citizens informed.

Get the "right" people at the table—One of the core goals of CPI was to shift from a culture of entitlement and dependence to one of self-reliance and independence. Broad civic engagement was essential to achieving this objective. From the initial kickoff and the very first visioning sessions in each community, fostering citizen participation has been a priority. A common theme was the importance of including young people. Our data suggest that the community recognizes that youth involvement is essential since the ultimate fate of the community rests in the hands of the next generation, and a number of the people interviewed saw a direct link between engaged teens and parent involvement.

Having the "right" people at the table was also essential in carrying the work forward. Even with vision, enthusiasm and commitment, if the people who can make it happen are not at the table, great ideas may never come to fruition.

Engage the responsible critic—The inclusivity advocated through CPI produced an unexpected multiplier effect. The synergistic results of "just getting together with people and talking about a common cause" produced benefits for everyone involved. Entrepreneurs gained access to advice and expertise that was not previously available. Local business owners learned more about niche opportunities that would allow them to expand and grow their businesses. And citizens had a venue and an audience to promote and celebrate the unique aspects of their communities. Of course, it is not always easy to be inclusive. Sometimes, in spite of massive effort, stimulating involvement can be a difficult task. Some may be apathetic, indifferent or disinterested. Others may be unaware or misinformed. And still others may be conflicted, concerned or outright opposed to a particular course of action. But true outreach engages responsible critics by listening to their concerns, focusing on common interests and encouraging involvement.

> Understanding the key elements of community culture, leadership, stability, empowerment, charitable giving as well as defining key roles for major players such as community foundations, government and local citizens will determine how communities thrive or fail in our global economy.

At least three things should be remembered when reaching out to those who have been unresponsive or critical. First, be patient—sometimes people just need time. Second, "meet people where they are." If the hope is to involve people from the mill, then go to the mill. If more youth involvement is needed, then be visible at the area high school. And finally, focus on common interests. People often did this by engaging in point-counterpoint-type discussions with those who professed a desire to produce some future outcome but were more intent on "looking at the top of their shoes" than doing something that might facilitate the expected results.

Be patient and stay the course—As noted previously, the kind of change proposed through CPI takes time. At least three things can be done to maintain momentum. First, continually develop local leadership. Recommendations here are consistent with the underlying assumptions that guide succession planning in business. Succession planning is an essential human resource function that ensures highly qualified people are throughout the organization today and into the future. When succession planning is done well, talented people are identified, mentored and trained to develop higher level and broader responsibilities.

Second, sometimes it is important to ask for help, particularly when the momentum seems to be slowing. This help can come in many forms. It can come from a guest speaker with experience directly relevant to a current issue or concern. It can take the form of a study tour to learn more about how others are responding to similar challenges. It can come from a hired consultant who can facilitate difficult conversations. The important thing is to ask for the help when needed.

And finally, celebrate success. "Celebrate every success… no matter how small the success…celebrate a little bit or a lot and people will want to stay involved."

One additional comment related to leadership; don't lead from above and don't assume you have all the answers. Leadership doesn't have to mean leading the meeting or the agenda, but rather leadership is about providing tools where necessary. This kind of leadership facilitates engagement and brings additional people around the table particularly because the ones at the table are apt to think either they need to make it happen or find the people who can. This kind of leadership also promotes broad ownership; no one is telling anyone else how to do it when what's being done is crafted by those who are ultimately affected.

And finally, surprising things that were not expected can happen. Give them the tools, and trust that the people will make the right decisions for the community.

Judith L. Millesen is Associate Professor of Political Science and a faculty fellow at the Voinovich School for Leadership and Public Affairs at Ohio University, Kenneth Strmiska is Managing Director for Community Foundation Services at the Council on Foundations and Martha Ahrendt is Vice President for Programs and Development at the Greater Green Bay Community Foundation. This essay is adapted from a longer academic paper by the authors prepared for the Helen Bader Institute for Nonprofit Management at the University of Wisconsin-Milwaukee. See www.progressinitiative.com for more information about the Community Progress Initiative.

CONCLUSION

S h e r e c e   Y .   W e s t

Rural America as Philanthropy's Frontier:
A Call for Increased Commitment

Like many, I am very familiar with images of poverty, squalor and hopelessness in the shadows of America's cities. The majority of my orientation as a funder has been formed by work in urban America. But serving as a funder in Louisiana and Arkansas over the past three years, I have discovered that dislocation, poverty and pain are as prevalent in rural communities as in any city.

I have also begun to wonder why the plight of rural communities is not more evident in the funding priorities of private foundations. Those of us funding in rural communities need philanthropic partners. We want to collaborate on long-term systemic change initiatives.

Rural America is the land of opportunity for philanthropy. It is a frontier for philanthropy to test assumptions, take risks, leverage dollars, influence public policy and learn lessons. We can support innovation and then disseminate information about the new programs, processes, knowledge, skills or concepts in play to improve the capacity of communities and organizations providing services and supports in rural America.

That's why this journal is such a historic document. It calls on our nation's philanthropic community to increase its commitment to rural America. The authors collectively respond to several compelling questions: Why increase philanthropy's commitment to rural America? What are the opportunities for supporting change in rural communities? And what would be the impact of such funding in rural communities? The authors successfully frame funding opportunities of national significance in rural communities. These funding opportunities work to address rural society's challenges by engaging its people, by building resilient communities and by developing a strong knowledge base for supporting long-term systemic change in rural America.

Rural America deserves philanthropy's attention. Our children, families and communities in rural America are suffering from poor education, health, wealth and other outcomes, contributing to a lack of social, economic and environmental progress. We should no longer neglect the needs and priorities of a rural America struggling to educate its children and employ its families.

It is important to state that this is in no way an urban funding versus rural funding debate. If we are to achieve positive outcomes for children, families and communities in America, we must increase grantmaking to rural America. We must go beyond our comfort and bias in support of urban America and provide additional resources to rural America to build its social, political, human and other capital to improve the lives of rural Americans. By 2015, philanthropy must work as diligently in rural communities as it does in urban communities. We must significantly increase grantmaking to address the priorities of rural America.

Philanthropy Must Provide Resources to Address the Issues Facing Rural America

Let's revisit what we mean by "rural America." In chapter one of this journal, Linda Reed notes that when you've seen one rural community, you've seen one rural community. In her essay in chapter two, Ivye Allen suggests that to determine whether an area is rural, "ask the locals—they'll tell you the correct answer." Neither author is just being cute. As Karl Stauber notes in chapter two, the federal government has six definitions of rural, from the Census Bureau's focus on population density to the Department of Agriculture's focus on an area's population and proximity to urban. Specifically, the USDA says that "rurality" includes "all places and people living outside the primary daily commuting zone of cities of 50,000 people or more." Based on this definition, latest estimates from the USDA indicate that approximately 50 million people live in rural areas, or nearly one in five Americans.

A common theme throughout this journal is that rural America contributes to all of America. According to a 2001 study of rural America supported by the W.K. Kellogg Foundation, respondents perceived that rural America helps perpetuate the values that define America, like individualism and self-sufficiency. Rural Americans are also perceived as the nation's backbone as the suppliers of food. Rural America contains the last vestiges of open space often targeted for a rapidly developing suburban landscape.

Respondents of the Kellogg study cite lack of money, price of crops and lack of opportunities as the most important problems facing rural America. Of greatest concern to those surveyed was the low agricultural profitability and job insecurity facing rural America. Also of concern were inadequate access to health care, along with few educational choices, opportunities for professional advancement and cultural resources.

In a 2004 analysis, the National Committee for Responsive Philanthropy identified fewer than 200 foundations actively engaged in grantmaking to rural areas and roughly $300 million in grants classified as rural—out of a total of more than 65,000 active foundations and $30 billion granted annually nationwide. In a report last August, the Center for Rural Strategies noted there's little evidence to suggest this has changed since. Furthermore, Michael Schechtman points out in chapter two of this journal that the "philanthropic divide," or gap in in-state foundation assets between those states with the least and those with the most, has nearly quadrupled between 1990 and 2007, to $36.1 billion. The result of this inattention and lack of investment in rural people and communities is very apparent and consistent with the perceptions of the respondents in the Kellogg study.

Raising these and other issues pertinent to people in rural America is important because, as Miriam Shark, Rachel Tompkins and Mario Gutierrez observe in their respective essays in chapter five, millions of children and families in rural America experience multiple "preventable deprivations," to quote Marian Wright Edelman of the Children's Defense Fund. That is, millions of children and families in rural America lack adequate health care and/or health insurance; lack enough food to stave off hunger; are legally homeless when they are doubled-up or tripled-up in a home or cannot find or afford housing; and lack safe and quality child care and after-school programs. Poor children in many rural communities are denied quality preschool to help them get ready for school. Millions more students coming out of some rural school systems cannot read or write, or are at risk of dropping out or being pushed out of school, resulting in fewer ready for college or for careers providing wages to sustain a family.

As Steve Gunderson said at the Council's conference last August in Missoula, Montana: "In the end, I do not believe we achieve these goals through a simple redistribution of existing philanthropy; rather, we do so by making a total commitment to grow philanthropy in rural America while growing philanthropy's role in service to the rural life we celebrate." Through philanthropy's collective wisdom and experience we can provide a clear vision, firm commitment and persistence to remove the barriers to enduring social change in rural America.

Now that I work as a funder with the farm belt in walking distance, I have seen first-hand that many children in rural America struggle to thrive in working-poor families. Their families often play by America's rules, expressing more patriotism and national pride than those in nearly any urban community, but still cannot earn a livable wage or compel sufficient support from local, state and national governments to escape intractable poverty cycles. The resulting discouragement and despair is familiar to urban funders. As a field, philanthropy has the unique capacity to be a catalytic resource that raises concern, highlights potential and fosters advocacy for rural communities. Philanthropy must provide resources to address issues facing rural America. Like previous authors in this journal, I too am confident that philanthropy can help to transform these devastating disparities and inequities to hope and healing. But whether the field will recognize that what happens positively or negatively in one part of America affects all of America—that remains an unanswered question.

Philanthropy Must Support Long-term Systemic Change Opportunities that Address the Priorities of Rural America

Peter Pennekamp, Janet Topolsky, James Richardson and Athan Lindsay point to a growing number of funders and social change agents taking bold action in rural communities to help tackle the grave social and environmental challenges to America's collective future. These funders and change agents, including the Nebraska Community Foundation and the McKnight Foundation-supported Minnesota Initiative Foundations, are becoming intentional about shifting structures, cultures and institutions. They are pioneering an emerging area of practice called Rural Development Philanthropy.

Such practices are not yet widespread in rural America. As mentioned earlier, rural America is fertile ground for initiatives of national significance that seek to address challenges for rural communities by engaging local people; by helping them to build resilient communities; and by increasing awareness and knowledge about the positive potential of strategic philanthropy. The mirrored needs of rural and urban communities also create an opportunity for philanthropy to create human linkages and dialogue across race, class and cultural divides. Philanthropy must support long-term systemic change opportunities that address the priorities of rural America.

Let's discuss some of these priorities.

Stem the rural brain drain—Anecdotally, we often hear of the exodus of young people, usually the best and the brightest, from rural areas who seldom return. Conversely, the young people who stay often do so because they cannot afford to leave—they don't have the opportunity. Whether these obvious social realities discourage and diminish expectations is unclear, but the average rural high school dropout rate of 19 percent (compared to 15 percent among urban schools) and rural residents' college completion rate of about 17 percent (compared to more than 29 percent of urban residents) suggest that generational poverty will continue in rural America. Also complicating matters: The Economic Research Service of the USDA reports that median weekly earnings for college graduates in 2006 were 24 percent higher in urban areas than in rural areas. Little wonder young people who can leave, do. Working to help convince them to stay, and others to return, will require stepped-up efforts, such as the Lumina Foundation's work (profiled in John Beineke and Martha Lamkin's essay in chapter five) to help youth prepare and succeed in college. Also required are workforce efforts to help rural residents earn more, such as those documented in Miriam Shark's essay in chapter five. This is a role tailor-made for philanthropy.

Replace the "philanthropic divide" with the "philanthropic tide"—When we talk about the "philanthropic divide" we often mean that giving by larger foundations disproportionately goes to urban and not rural areas. This picture is changing thanks to the work of the community foundations and community-based giving traditions that are creating a new tide of "place-based" philanthropy in which those who live and work in rural areas are investing in the future of their own communities. Further, community foundations are the dominant type of funder in rural America. We must support and build the grantmaking capacity of community foundations. Community foundations are excellent vehicles to act as catalytic hubs for supporting the long-term systemic change many rural communities are seeking. For large foundations without the capacity to deploy staff to work directly in rural communities, community foundations—as well as other funding intermediaries—are the agents of change. Rural America is increasingly in search of resources to build its community philanthropy capacity—a role tailor-made for philanthropy.

Move from adversity to diversity—Many of us are familiar with stereotypes of rural America. Such stereotypes do not usually evoke the folksy empathy of Garrison Keillor's "News from Lake Wobegon" reports from *A Prairie Home Companion*. Rather, we are likely to dismiss the needs and opinions of people and communities that we may assume to be backwards, culturally isolated and even bigoted. Culture, class and racial barriers exist here, just as they exist in the rest of America. But rural America is also experiencing increased diversification due to economic necessity. If many rural communities are to survive, they must attract and retain both the labor and civic participation of new people and maximize the engagement of all of their residents. As a result, rural America is increasingly in search of approaches to develop inclusive leadership structures and broader civic participation—a role tailor-made for philanthropy.

Move to healthy, wealthy and wise—Health, economic development and education continue to be major issues that funders working in rural areas must address. To improve outcomes in these and other critical indicators of child, family and community well-being, philanthropy should work with rural communities to develop strategies to positively address the factors and to measure progress. Moreover, philanthropy will need to think differently about the pathways and models to deliver services and supports and to achieve results. For example, hospitals are far and few between in many rural communities. Building a network of community-based health workers to deliver quality health care services may be the most efficient way to deliver health services. Another example: It is highly improbable that rural communities will attract large manufacturing plants or other types of large-scale employers paying livable wages to most of the residents in the community. Thus, small- to medium-size businesses are major employers in rural America. To support them, investments need to be made in culture and asset-based entrepreneurship. A final example is that of workforce development, which must be supported in rural America to decrease the number of poorly educated young people entering the penal system. Rural America is in desperate need of strategies, approaches, lessons learned and more to address these factors—another role tailor-made for philanthropy.

Move from "programs and priorities" to "places and people"—The idea that funders can isolate their funding in silos and programmatic priorities and still manage to adequately address the needs of our communities is outdated. Exceptional work at making a difference builds upon the distinctive set of institutions, geographies and opportunities specific to each community and region. At the Annie E. Casey Foundation, I learned from its place-based community change work like *Making Connections* and the Rebuilding Communities Initiative that achieving sustainable results requires four things: (1) *Authentic demand* from residents and others not normally at the decision-making table; (2) *Committed allies* within and across the faith community, business sector, community organizations and government who champion the work and can "make things happen"; (3) *Dedicated resources*, including dollars but also data and volunteers; and (4) *Vigorous leadership* that can replenish and sustain itself over time. Rural America is increasingly in search of approaches to place-based sustainable change—a role tailor-made for philanthropy.

Naturally, as funders address these indicators, they will run up against barriers, such as a lack of capacity in nonprofit organizations, political or institutional resistance to change, or a lack of resources affecting a community's ability to sustain the innovation. These challenges are familiar to philanthropy. Barriers notwithstanding, finding long-term solutions is necessary to challenge existing systems and will demand new skills, relationships and mindsets. Philanthropy should be the catalyst for change in dysfunctional, ineffective systems.

Philanthropy Can and Must Do Better to Improve Outcomes in Rural America

Philanthropy should highlight the opportunities to make a difference in rural America. Urban America and rural America have the same legacy with twin affects. Lack of investment and ignoring the needs of the poor anywhere in this country opens them to fall prey to negative child and family well-being outcomes. Holding government accountable for providing services and supports to rural communities is as vitally important. Philanthropy has to provide the resources to highlight the needs of children and families in rural communities.

Now that I am exposed to the needs of rural America, I more deeply appreciate the passion that the late Dr. Martin Luther King Jr. brought to the issues affecting the poor in America. In 1967-1968, Dr. King launched a Poor People's Campaign to bring attention to rural communities and to raise the voices of the disempowered. The promise of that campaign was cut short.

Admittedly, when I was at Casey I did not pay a lot of attention to rural communities. Now that I have been working in rural communities for a short while, I am confident that there is a role for philanthropy to make the priorities of rural communities and the inequities experienced by millions of people transparent. I also find myself wondering why funding in rural areas does not seem as sexy as funding in urban areas. Do some people actually think that people in rural communities are less deserving of philanthropy's attention? Some may assert that you get more bang for your buck, media attention and economies of scale funding in urban areas. But I question the efficacy and morality of a philanthropy guided purely by such a cost-benefit analysis. It's a type of approach that deepens the neglect shown to Native Americans, African Americans, Latinos and others struggling to thrive in rural areas.

Philanthropy has the resources to fund advocacy and public policy to bring issues to light. Rural areas are lacking the philanthropic community to build organizational capacity and empower residents to influence public policy and influence how public resources are spent in their community. Yet despite what we know, it remains exceedingly challenging to encourage philanthropy to invest in community revitalization, workforce development, school readiness, child health and other initiatives that intentionally and explicitly address the formation of social capital, political capital, human capital and more that are critical to achieving better outcomes for vulnerable children and families. We have remained categorical in our thinking, our funding, our practice and our policy, despite all the evidence that tells us we have to connect the dots between building civic muscle through positive social networks, robust civic engagement, strong resident leaders and sustaining comprehensive social change. In our multifaceted roles as funders it is important that we highlight the opportunities to influence social change in rural America.

> If philanthropy continues to not invest in rural America, we send the message that rural America does not matter. If we do not get clearer about the strategies and approaches that are most effective in addressing social, economic and environmental change in rural America, we will continue to send the message that citizens of rural America are not worthy of philanthropy's support.

If we do not make investments in building the capacity of rural America to address its priorities, the capacity will not grow. If philanthropy continues to not invest in rural America, we send the message that rural America does not matter. If we do not get clearer about the strategies and approaches that are most effective in addressing social, economic and environmental change in rural America, we will continue to send the message that citizens of rural America are not worthy of philanthropy's support. Why not invest in Wyoming, Mississippi and Nebraska, or in rural areas of California and Florida? Is it because many of us are more comfortable funding in urban areas?

Is it our duty as funders to maximize our comfort? As I understand history, Congress allowed private money to be set aside tax-free in charitable foundations with the specific intent of creating funds providing additional support to help further the public good. By 2015, we need to think beyond our comfort and work to build the political, social, human and other capital necessary to effect change in rural America; to further the rural public good. It's a role tailor-made for philanthropy.

Sherece Y. West is President and CEO of the Winthrop Rockefeller Foundation in Little Rock, Arkansas. She previously served as CEO of the Louisiana Disaster Recovery Foundation and as a Program Associate at the Annie E. Casey Foundation.

APPENDIX I

Funding Recommendations in Key Rural Issue Areas

Report from Council on Foundations'
First Rural Philanthropy Conference

In August 2007, the Council on Foundations along with the Montana Community Foundation, the Northwest Area Foundation and others convened a Conference on Philanthropy and Rural America: A 21st Century Agenda. As part of this conference, various working groups identified their key recommendations and ideas for growing philanthropy's role in building a better quality of life in rural America. The following represent the specific recommendations of each of the working groups, listed in alphabetical order.

Arts and Culture

- Research and disseminate appropriate models for supporting rural arts and culture in rural America.

- The Council should incorporate the perspectives of arts and culture into each topic area of it work to boost philanthropy for rural America. Doing so will expand the understanding of how arts and culture helps to advance each sector's goals, not just those specific to arts and culture.

- For all arts funders and partners: learn what funding mechanisms are available to arts as entrepreneurs and the arts industry as a whole.

- Grantmakers in the Arts should seek to move the discussion of the Rural Agenda forward in order to expand the dialogue for all topic areas in rural America, and include other affinity groups in the discussion when possible.

Community Philanthropy

- Conduct transfer of wealth studies nationwide for every county in every state. Also, develop and distribute guides on the utilization of the resulting data to grow endowments in each county.

- Promote the use of low-profit limited liability companies (L3Cs), and other ways to leverage foundation assets.

- Pass the L3C bill in North Carolina or another state legislature and educate Congress about the possible use of L3Cs in legislation at the federal level.

- Identify the rural policy groups already in existence in order to utilize their expertise and engage them in developing the agenda for the 21st century.

- Assemble a rural community philanthropy steering group to develop an agenda and strategy to advance the field of "rural community philanthropy as a community change agent." The goal: become an affinity group of the Council.

- The Council on Foundations and the philanthropic sector accept their leadership roles as the connectors between rural America and all relevant sectors that have an impact on the issues of rural philanthropy, including Congress, the FDIC, the Federal Reserve; as well as state legislatures and the private sector.

Economic Development

- Pass the L3C bill at the state and federal levels.

- Document other vehicles like the L3C to benefit rural America.

- Build new rural capacity to do regional development and discovering and implementing funding for rural economic development work.

- Address the mismatch issue across the philanthropic spectrum of short-term versus long-term funding of projects.

- Form a Council Rural Economic Development Working Group, or link with an existing ongoing effort.

- Build a national fund for starting work on compelling issues.

- Begin building capacity to do rural economic development.

Education

- Develop community engagement and public support from policymakers to parents in the education of rural America's children.

- Replicate successful ideas through funding demonstration projects.

- Support community-based alternatives for children and youth to learn, and that also support learning especially when parental support is lacking.

- Each foundation working in education should issue reports, hold convenings, or in some other way raise awareness regarding the key issues in rural education, to create a buzz.

- Identify funders, and provide professional development grants to teachers in rural America.

Environment and Natural Resources

- Encourage grantmaking that marries environmental protection and restoration with community economic development. (For example, community and landscape-scale demonstrations and targeted initiatives.)

- Take advantage of growing interest in locally grown, healthy food systems; support messaging and outreach that bridges the differences between rural and urban.

- Invest in innovative technologies and in policy development to maximize local community benefits while rapidly increasing renewable low-carbon energy production.

- Fund more long-term collaborations that are cross-disciplinary in projects around the environment, health, community and economic development. Many of today's best innovations come from these collaborative processes.

Growing Philanthropy

- To grow philanthropy in rural America, organized philanthropy can facilitate community transformations and develop leadership, as well as addressing the issues of race, class and power.

- Conduct and publish the transfer of wealth study now for all 50 states, with the 10-year shelf life that reveals opportunities and demonstrates the sense of urgency this data provides.

- Build capacity in rural organizations—build networks to utilize these needs. Philanthropy needs to expand the networks beyond the traditional rural institutions most commonly associated with these discussions.

Health and Wellness

- Assess the impacts of the 2007 Farm Bill on rural communities and small farmers.

- Engage foundations to develop policy options to promote universal health care at the state level.

- Conduct a national assessment of broadband deployment and rural coverage.

- Work towards universal health care at the federal level.

- Convince Senator Baucus to call for a commission whose mission will be to redefine "rural" in all federal programs.

Housing

- Build the capacity of rural community developers and rural communities to address the housing needs in rural communities.

- Develop standardized tools and metrics to evaluate and identify local community housing needs as well as housing capacity.

Individual and Family Assets

- Launch the L3C initiative to focus on alternative financial services to rural Americans. Assist in the passage of the bill in North Carolina, or in another state. Also, secure a Congressional mandate to require the IRS to approve nationwide approval.

- Channel more support for innovative financial services and products such as the L3Cs, Shorebanks, Southern Bancorps, MACED, ECD and AFCU.

- Create a funding pool of $1 million to match operating funds for fuel-efficient, late-model cars purchased through Individual Development Accounts.

- Hold a second rural philanthropy conference with an agenda built in advance by practitioner-working groups, which will be responsible for reporting on the progress made in one year's time.

- Assure that rural and underserved areas get attention at the "Philanthropy's Vision: A Leadership Summit."

- Rebuild and strengthen the Rural Funders Network.

Technology

- Do the research required to discover which foundations fund technology in the grantmaking community and which public entities are involved.

- Leverage existing policies, such as the e-rate.

- Build alliances. Survey foundations interested in or currently funding telecommunications infrastructure in communities or community foundations.

- Technology's infrastructure in rural America requires a huge commitment by numerous actors, and cannot be accomplished without the commitment from the many sectors needed to achieve optimum results. This includes commitments from the investment, research, policy and implementation sectors.